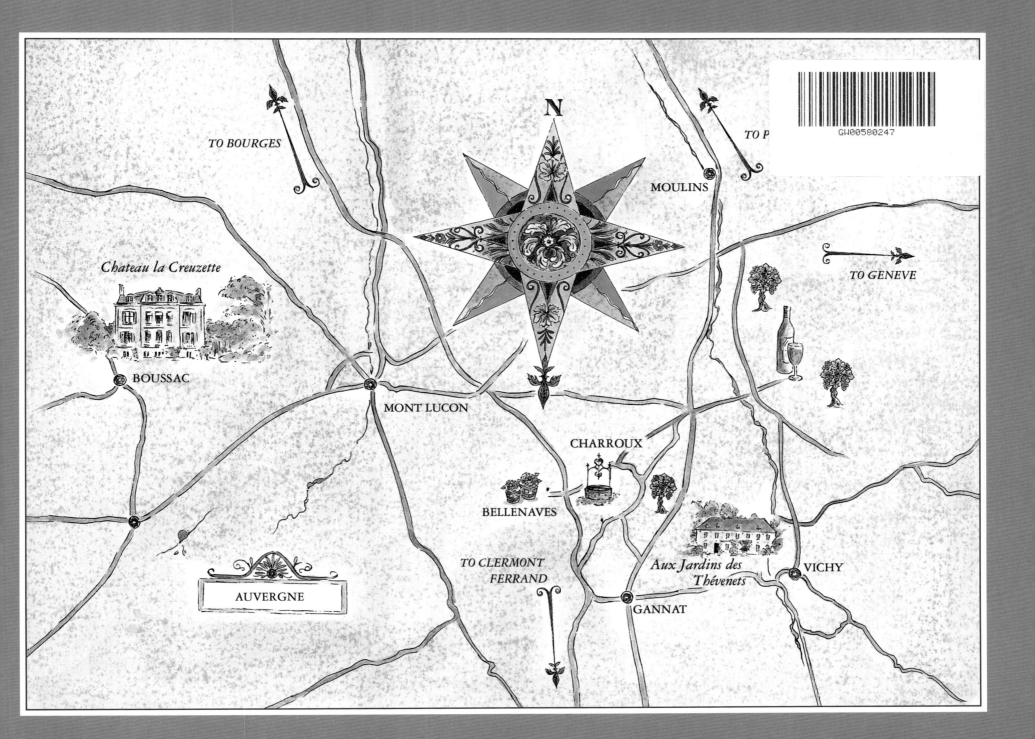

N

TO BOURGES

Chateau la Creuzette

MOULINS

TO P...

TO GENEVE

BOUSSAC

MONT LUCON

CHARROUX

BELLENAVES

TO CLERMONT FERRAND

Aux Jardins des Thévenets

VICHY

AUVERGNE

GANNAT

ACKNOWLEDGEMENTS

This book is for my remarkable husband and best friend, Deon, and my truly fabulous son, Renier.

I would like to thank the following people, without whom the journey that comprised this book would not have been possible: the owners of Chateau la Creuzette, Hardy Olivier and Louis Jansen van Vuuren; Olivier and Lynn Chaulieu, from Aux Jardin des Thévenets; Christof and LZ Albertyn, of Brandfontein; and Ben and Jeanneret Momberg, of Middelvlei.

To Stephen Inggs, *Delectable's* brilliant photographer, who had the guts to climb on a plane to France to help realise someone else's dream - thanks a lot.

Thank you, Chef John Jackson, for not only letting me loose in your kitchens, but also for agreeing to write the foreword to this book. It is an honour.

Thank you very much to Charl Mouton for your enthusiasm and creative input.

I want to thank Joyce Melani, who took complete control and responsibility for organising the rest of my world whilst the book was happening.

Also thanks to my friend Heather Parker, who agreed to copy-edit *Delectable*.

Thank you René de Wet for your insight with the design of the book.

And then there is Basil van Rooyen who took the entire package from my hands with absolute confidence and huge tact, and had it published.

The most heartfelt thanks goes to the two most important people in my life, Deon and Renier. You two gentlemen supported me unconditionally... and coped almost too well while I've been away for weeks at a time! Thank you.

My generous parents, Patens and Petro van Rooyen, and my siblings taught me that the best times in one's life are spent around a table with family and friends misbehaving noisily. It is wonderful to be part of this crazy family.

And it goes almost without saying that the stunning friends we have in Cape Town all contributed with their support and care.

I'm long overdue in inviting you all for a long, leisurely lunch. Soon!

Thanks to you all.
Marlene van der Westhuizen

The first edition of *Delectable* was published jointly by Rollerbird Press, a division of Troupant Publishers (Pty) Limited and Pan Macmillan SA (Pty) Limited.

ISBN 978-1-920434-09-0

First edition, third impression 2011

Published jointly by
Bookstorm (Pty) Limited, Suite 10, Private Bag X12, Cresta, 2118, Johannesburg, South Africa, www.bookstorm.co.za
and Pan Macmillan South Africa, Private Bag X19, Northlands, 2116, South Africa, www.panmacmillan.co.za

Distributed by Pan Macmillan via Booksite Africa

Edited by Heather Parker
Cover design and layout by René de Wet
Printed by Ultra Litho

Delectable

FOOD FROM RURAL FRANCE TO URBAN CAPE

Delectable

FOOD FROM RURAL FRANCE TO URBAN CAPE

MARLENE VAN DER WESTHUIZEN · PHOTOGRAPHY BY STEPHEN INGGS

BOOK**STORM**

MACMILLAN

Contents

Foreword

Sometimes dynamite really does come in small, if glamorous, packages, as I discovered when the petite Marlene van der Westhuizen exploded, in the nicest possible way, into the kitchens of my Cape Town restaurant, wanting to train to be a chef.

Little did I then realise just how good she was going to be, or what good friends we would become, just how passionate she was about cooking, or how far her cooking would take her. Or that she was fearless. It came to mind one day that it must have been a male chef who coined the phrase 'if you can't stand the heat, get out of the kitchen' when I found Marlene in the Cold Room in tears, taking refuge from some truly chauvinistic chefs. They only tried it once: the dynamite exploded, along with a few choice words, and the chefs realised it would be better not to mess with this pint-sized bundle of determination. From then on she became 'one of the boys' in charge and cooked up a storm.

One of the particular joys of my restaurant was hosting top European chefs for seasons of their cooking. One of these hailed from Alsace, and who did he choose to work in his Michelin-starred restaurant? In this way Marlene cemented an earlier fascination with all things French, while never forgetting her love of the Cape.

Now, eight years later, Marlene is everywhere. Cooking all over South Africa for the high flying and the adored. Judging cookery demonstrations as Vice Conseiller Culinaire of the Chaine des Rotisseurs in the Western Cape. Writing for magazines, giving cookery classes... glass of wine in hand... in her charming home in Green Point Village, or for three years at the Chateau la Creuzette in France, for troops of South Africans who soon learn to march to the beat of Marlene's enthusiastic culinary drum. And, now, unsurprisingly, publishing a book that is as original a creation as its author. All the while renovating a gem of a four-level house in Charroux, officially one of the crown jewels of romantic French villages, supported by her hunky husband Deon - Marlene *does* only choose the finest ingredients in everything she does! - and strapping teenage son Renier.

Marlene's delectable first-born (I am sure many other 'children' will follow) is ten chapters of her remarkable culinary and lifestyle experiences, not of Cape to Cairo, but far sexier Cape to Charroux! With some achingly beautiful detours on the way, brilliantly photographed by Stephen Inggs.

The chapter titles tell you immediately that this is not another cookery book that will gather dust on bookstore shelves among rows of less original printed cousins. From buzzy Green Point Village to wild, wonderful Brandfontein near Cape Agulhas, eight dazzling French vignettes with evocative names like the Chateau la Creuzette or Aux Jardins des Thévenets, it's a catalogue of pure entertainment. Marlene's writing makes you feel you have been to the Wednesday Market at Bellenaves or the Brocante on a Sunday, while having a romantic fling in Paris. So many disparate elements one might think, and how will she pull them all together in one book? As you will read, effortlessly and seamlessly.

Delectable is a genuine five-star Michelin original, a very different take on the finer things of life, that will bring readers around Marlene's extravagant but honest table, with deep flavoured food matched with the romance of fine bottles of wine about to be opened and enjoyed, along with good fellowship, laughter and grand companions. There are homes and kitchens of rare beauty as she pulls you into her world of two of the most gorgeous corners of the earth.

If the gods punish those they love by granting them all their wishes, then Marlene is in big trouble... but the reader will be able to see her with a wooden ladle in one hand stirring a copper pot, a glass of noble merlot in the other as she winks at them.

All the recipes are original Marlene interpretations, reflecting her connecting of the Cape with the Auvergne. Cook them! Enjoy them! They're delectable! And so is she!

JOHN JACKSON
Royal Malewane, Thornybush Private Game Reserve
South Africa, 2006

Introduction

The idea for this cookbook was born late one evening around the kitchen table at Chateau la Creuzette. It is a natural decision after having numerous groups of people from South Africa visiting and cooking in the beautiful rustic kitchens of the Chateau.... They all leave for home having started a lifelong love affair with France, and its food- and wine-orientated lifestyle. And they have a completely new take on cheese and antique linen!

This is a compilation of some of the recipes I've demonstrated both in South Africa and France over the last three years... shot on location at Chateau la Creuzette, Boussac village, Charroux village and the beautiful guest farm, Aux Jardin des Thévenets. These magical spots can be found in the Auvergne... an awesome place of green rolling fields, deep gorges and still running rivers. And also the home of Charolais cattle... think osso buco, wonderful cheese, mushrooms, wild boar, mustard and the oldest vineyard in France, St Pourcain.

The style of cooking in this book is not exclusively French... more what I fondly call 'brasserie luxe', simple food that looks as good as it tastes - and do remember to taste! For this book to be representative of all the things I love most, I had to include the three places in the Western Cape that I cannot imagine living without: Green Point Village in Cape Town, where I live with my family; Middelvlei Wine Estate in Stellenbosch, where I have on numerous occasions cooked up a storm; and Brandfontein, close to L'Agulhas, which is arguably the most beautiful, unspoiled place in the world.

I've made sure that the produce I mention, however exotic it seems, is readily available in most of the local supermarkets or delis. Enjoy the food and fabulous pictorials. And 'perchance to dream'... a soupçon?

MARLENE VAN DER WESTHUIZEN
Cape Town, 2006

CHAPTER 1

OOKING AT LA CREUZETTE

The best way to approach Chateau la Creuzette in the village of Boussac, is by foot. Walking through the huge stone gateposts and up the ancient tree lined, slightly musty smelling road towards the imposing front door, with the morning's still-warm baguettes under your arm, does set the stage for a perfect stay.

And if you should fill your time with elegant dinners around the dramatic table in the main dining room, long slow suppers in the kitchen underneath the artist's studio, or seriously noisy cooking demonstrations with palate-blowing winetastings, you would have done well!

The fare at La Creuzette whenever I was in charge of the kitchen was rustic, real food. Heaps of it... No menu in the Auvergne can be complete without the truly French classics like gigot or leg of lamb, canard or duck and, naturally, tarte tatin or apple tart. The recipes I have included here are all redolent of cherished times past. What a pleasure that with the aromas and textures of this food one could capture a memory... ⚜

LEFT: *The dark, blood-red roses underneath the 'Grande Salon' window have a completely heady aroma...*

Gougères

In the south of France, these are served as a snack with a glass of sauvignon blanc... I find them not too shabby with a little chardonnay either! This makes enough for 12.

- 125 g butter, diced
- ½ t salt
- pinch cayenne pepper
- pinch grated nutmeg
- 115 g plain flour, sifted
- 4 eggs
- 115 g strong-tasting cheese, diced (in France, I use Comté Gruyère)

Preheat the oven to 200°C/Gas 6. Pour 250 ml water in a saucepan, heat on the stove, and melt the butter in it. Add the salt, cayenne pepper and nutmeg and bring to the boil. Remove from the heat, and add the flour all at once, beating well, until the mixture pulls away from the side of the pan.

Leave to cool slightly, then whisk in the eggs, one at a time. Whisk until glossy and thick. Fold in the diced cheese.

Drop the mixture into well-greased muffin pans. Bake for 20 minutes, then lower the temperature to 180°C/Gas 4, and bake for a further 15 minutes until golden. Leave to cool slightly - you don't want to burn the fingers now, do you? - and serve.

FAR LEFT: *Something to read...*
LEFT: *The gougères, being made with choux pastry, drop really fast after you've taken them from the oven. Make haste!*
Recommended wine: The Right Two Whites

Leg of lamb with anchovies, garlic & rosemary

This is a remarkably subtle and beautiful combination. Do not be put off by the quantities of garlic.
When cooked, it is a gentle purée! Serves 8.

- 1 leg of lamb
- 500 g garlic, about a third of it peeled and cut in slivers, and the rest left whole
- 9 anchovy fillets, halved
- 18 sprigs rosemary
- 175 ml lamb stock

FAR LEFT: *An entire leg of lamb slow roasting in a built-in fireplace.*
LEFT: *A drawer full of silver.*
Recommended wine: Plaisier de Merle Merlot

Make 18 small slits in the lamb, and stuff each with a sliver of garlic, half an anchovy and a sprig of rosemary.

Preheat your oven to 200°C/Gas 6. Place a roasting rack in a roasting pan, put the meat uncovered on top of the rack and roast for one hour. The meat should be cooked but still slightly pink in the middle when you slice it.

While the meat is cooking, blanch the rest of the garlic cloves in boiling water for about five minutes. Drain, put on a piece of foil onto which you've smeared some olive oil, season, and put in the oven with the lamb for 30 minutes. Remove the garlic from the oven. Squeeze the now fabulously soft purée out of the cloves into a saucepan and add the lamb stock. If there are any pan juices in the roasting pan, add those as well. Gently reduce the sauce until it has a thick, creamy consistency.

Serve the sliced leg on a large platter with baby potatoes in the skin. And of course serious amounts of the garlic cream!

ABOVE: *Lunch and a glass of wine outside the chateau kitchen.*

LEFT: *Roasted pears.*

Roasted pears with asparagus & green beans

This salad is a firm favourite during summer lunches as either a starter, or served after the main course.
I sometimes add a little ripe blue cheese... excellent with the pears. Serves 6.

- 3 firm, ripe pears
- 100 ml extra virgin olive oil
- 20 g castor sugar
- 600 g young green beans, topped and tailed
- 30 green asparagus spears
- 100 g walnuts, roasted and chopped

Dressing
- 50 ml walnut oil
- 10 ml honey
- 50 ml cream
- 1 t smooth mustard
- 1 clove garlic, peeled and finely chopped
- salt and pepper to taste

Preheat the oven to 180°C/Gas 4. Halve the pears, skin on, and cut each half into thirds. Line up the pear slices in a roasting pan, drizzle with 30 ml olive oil and sprinkle the castor sugar over evenly. Bake for 20 minutes until the pears have coloured slightly, but are still crunchy.

Meanwhile, pour a little cold water into a shallow frying pan. Add the beans and the asparagus, and bring to a gentle, happy boil. Do not cover - this will help to retain the bright green of the vegetables. Remove from the heat after 5 minutes - the vegetables must still be crunchy. Drain and immediately toss 20 ml olive oil into the warm beans and asparagus. Season lightly.

In the meantime, make the creamy vinaigrette dressing by shaking together the remaining olive oil, the walnut oil, the cream, mustard, garlic, and salt and pepper.

Allow the beans, asparagus and pears to cool. Add the walnuts and vinaigrette, and toss the salad. Serve.

ABOVE: *Golden Delicious apples.*

RIGHT: *I bake the tarte tatin in a really old flan dish which I found on the brocante (antique market).*

Tarte tatin

The most wonderful apple tart known to man! And you can still order it at Maxim's in Paris where it is a speciality to this day. The Tatin sisters ran a restaurant in Lamotte-Beuvron at the beginning of last century and, according to legend, one of the old girls dropped the tart as she was putting it in the oven... hence baking it upside down, with the absolutely delicious result of butter, sugar and apple juices all coming together in the most divine caramel. I just love this story and am constantly dropping stuff in the hope... Serves 10 (or one, when nobody is looking).

- 125 g unsalted butter, diced
- 11 Golden Delicious apples, peeled, each sliced into six wedges
- 550 g castor sugar
- 125 ml crème fraîche
- 1 roll puff pastry, thawed

Use a tablespoon of the butter to grease a baking tray, and neatly pack the sliced apple wedges onto the tray. Sprinkle 50 g castor sugar evenly over the apple wedges and bake/dry them in a moderate oven, 180°C/Gas 4, for about 1½ hours, or until the apples turn a light caramel colour. Remove them from the tray swiftly - they tend to stick!

Meanwhile, melt the rest of the castor sugar in a saucepan with 2 T water. Wait until the caramel boils in lovely, big bubbles before you add the crème fraîche. Beware of the steam! Keep stirring until the extra moisture has reduced, then stir the butter into the sauce. It keeps the caramel from becoming too sticky.

Pour the caramel into a round springform cake tin, and let it cool to room temperature. Pack the apple wedges on/into the caramel in overlapping concentric circles.

Cover the fruit with the pastry, tucking it under the edge of the cake tin. Prick with a fork. Put the tin onto a baking tray... the tart tends to leak a little... and bake for 45 minutes at 200°C/Gas 6, or until the pastry turns a golden, caramel colour.

Remove from the oven and tip the baking tin deftly - don't burn yourself! Serve still slightly warm with a dollop of cream.

ABOVE: *The back entrance to the park around Chateau la Creuzette has a rustic charm.*

Marrow bones on toast

What is life without the marrow…? Serve with a flourish and a glass of robust red! Serves 6 richly.

- 12 slices white bread
- 12 thick-cut marrow bones
- 1 ℓ chicken stock
- salt and freshly milled black pepper

Put the marrow bones on their sides in a pot - that way, the marrow won't fall out during cooking. Cover with water and bring to the boil. Boil the bones for about 5 minutes, then pour the water off, refill the pot with fresh water, and bring to the boil again. Repeat the process once more, but the third time, rather than water, pour the chicken stock over the bones and bring to the boil. Boil for 10 minutes this time, then remove the bones from the pot, leaving the stock to reduce. Remove the pot from the heat once the stock has been reduced by three quarters.

Toast the bread, and arrange two slices each on a small plate. Spoon the marrow on top, and pour some of the reduced stock over. Season to taste and serve immediately.

ABOVE: *Front door detail.*

Recommended wine: Bosman Kabinet

Heather's roasted ginger & thyme duck

Ducks are widely available at good butcheries. One of the best things about this recipe, is that you'll have jars and jars of lovely duck fat to keep in your fridge to use later... great for braising meat before stewing it. My dear friend, Heather, served this one windless evening on her rooftop patio overlooking Cape Town harbour... unforgettable! Had to bribe her to get the recipe. Serves 4.

- 2 ducks (about 1,5 kg each)
- 150 g fresh ginger, sliced
- 2 leeks, sliced
- 2 carrots, chopped in large chunks
- 4 cloves garlic
- 20 sprigs thyme
- 4 firm pears, halved and peeled
- 250 ml red wine
- 250 ml chicken stock
- seasoning

ABOVE RIGHT: *Fresh ginger.*
Recommended wine: La Cave Merlot, slightly chilled

Rinse the ducks and pat dry with a paper towel. Season with sea salt and milled black pepper. Combine the ginger, leeks, carrots, garlic and thyme, and use this to stuff the ducks. Place the ducks on the rack of a roasting pan, and pour water into the pan, to just below the level of the rack. Cover tightly with foil and roast/steam for 45 minutes at 220°C/Gas 7.

Remove from the oven and turn it down to 200°C/Gas 6. Remove the foil, pour off the liquid into a bowl, and set the liquid to cool. Return the ducks to the oven, and roast uncovered for another 45 minutes. They are ready when they are crisp and a lovely caramel colour. In the meantime, peel and core the pears. Skim some of the duck fat off the bowl and into a pan and braise the pears in the fat over medium heat for 5 minutes. Remove from the pan, sprinkle with black pepper, and keep both pears and pan aside.

Remove the ducks from the oven, scoop out the stuffing, and add it to the pan, along with the red wine. Set the ducks aside to rest, and bring the contents of the pan to a rapid boil. Let the liquid reduce by half, scoop the solids out, add the chicken stock, and reduce again to the saucy, yummy stage... if you don't know what that looks like, call me.

Arrange a breast, leg and thigh per serving on mashed potatoes, pasta or couscous; add a pear to each serving. Pour the reduced sauce over the dish and garnish with thyme.

LEFT: *I received these cups from a generous Madame at an antique market after buying some French linen from her. They are absolutely perfect for this dish.*

ABOVE: *The deep pink of the Souvenir de Louis Amade.*

Heavenly chocolate cups

This is a truly French dessert. Serve with caution: no-one can be held responsible for their actions after this. And yes, it's really rich. Makes 10 small portions.

- 500 ml thick cream
- 250 g quality dark chocolate, broken into little pieces
- 5 egg yolks, beaten
- zest of one orange, finely grated

Put the cream and chocolate into a pot, and stir over medium heat until the cream is warm enough to cause the chocolate to melt. Take off the heat and cool slightly before folding in the egg yolks. Add the zest.

Pour into small, pretty ramekins and refrigerate. Serve with red berries.

'If one had the choice of again hearing Pachmann play the two Chopin sonatas or dining once more at the Café Anglais, which would one choose?' ALICE B. TOKLAS

ABOVE RIGHT: *Beautiful roses in silver.*
BELOW RIGHT: *The back view of Chateau la Creuzette.*

Lentil & mushroom soup

Lentils have a dull-but-worthy reputation. It's time to get over that. This soup is amazing - and Puy lentils are increasingly easy to find at delis. Serves 8.

- 300 g Puy lentils, simmered in 600 ml water until tender (about 30 min)
- 1 onion, finely chopped
- 100 ml duck fat or olive oil
- 2 cloves garlic, chopped
- 1 large potato, peeled and diced
- 600 g mushrooms, chopped into tiny pieces
- 500 ml chicken stock
- sea salt and freshly ground black pepper

Sauté the onion in fat or oil for 3-4 min. Add the garlic, potato and mushroom, cover, and sweat for a few minutes. Stir well. When the lentils are tender, tip the mushroom mixture into the lentil pot and add the stock. Bring to a simmer and season. Blend the soup with a handheld blender. Reheat and serve very hot with persillade or a dollop of tapenade.

ABOVE RIGHT: *Wrought iron detail at Chateau la Creuzette.*
BELOW RIGHT: *Door to the castle!*

Blue cheese tart with phyllo pastry

This tart was first made for me years ago as a light supper before a rather weighty opera and I've never quite got over it. Serves 8.

- 4 sheets phyllo pastry
- 10 ml butter, melted
- 2 celery sticks, chopped thinly
- 250 g Roquefort, crumbled
- 125 ml cream
- 2 eggs, whisked
- milled black pepper to taste

Preheat the oven to 180°C/Gas 4.

Brush the melted butter gently over the sheets of phyllo. Place the sheets, one on top of the other at an angle, in a buttered tart dish. Fry the celery in a little leftover butter until it is lightly cooked. Remove the pan from the heat, and stir the cheese, cream, eggs and pepper into the celery. Pour the mixture into the phyllo pastry case and, using your fingers, mould the pastry to your liking... prettily or artistically!... before putting it in the oven for around 35 minutes, or until the phyllo turns a light caramel colour and the filling has set. Serve warm with rocket and a dollop of quince jelly.

ABOVE: *Kitchen steps... a wonderful perch from which to contemplate the day ahead while sipping your coffee.*
Recommended wine: Meerlust Merlot, slightly chilled

 COUNTRY KITCHEN

Trying to avoid the cold morning dew on your ankles by slipping your feet into a pair of oversized wellies on your way to the chicken coop, is par for the course at Chateau la Creuzette. And returning to the huge, stone-walled kitchen with a basket of fresh eggs is also normal. The next step is to stroll through the herb and vegetable garden to stock up on produce for the day's cooking class. From an assortment of berries to leeks, from baby tomatoes and red peppers to herbs, it's all there.

Back behind the chopping block later in the day, with a glass of wine at your elbow and Jane Birkin crooning in the background, the serious prep starts. And it feels like art. ⚜

LEFT: *An old, restored barn next to the chateau now houses the demonstration kitchen.*

Cauliflower soup with truffle oil

I was inspired by John Burton Race's French Leave *programme on BBC. It's superb - and this recipe finally overturns the English reputation for killing the cruciferous vegetable family... the lingering smell of which can still be found in some of the colonies. Serves 8.*

- 100 g salted butter
- 1 kg fresh cauliflower, trimmed and broken into florets
- 3 leeks, peeled, chopped and rinsed
- 4 cloves garlic, chopped
- 3 sprigs fresh thyme, plus an extra sprig per serving for garnish
- 2 bay leaves
- 800 ml chicken stock
- 125 ml full cream
- truffle oil

Melt the butter in a soup pot and add the cauliflower pieces, stirring them into the butter. Add the leeks, garlic, thyme and bay leaves, and fry lightly. Add stock to the vegetables and bring to a slow, pleasant boil. Keep this going until the cauliflower is soft. Remove the bay leaves and thyme sticks from the pot, and liquidise the soup. Reheat gently, stir in the cream, spoon into lovely, large soup plates, and add a drop of truffle oil to each bowl. Garnish with a sprig of thyme, and serve this gorgeous soup with some crusty bread.

ABOVE FAR LEFT: *An ancient chopping block... and leeks from the vegetable and herb garden.*
ABOVE RIGHT: *Wonderful, irreplaceable truffle oil!*

A COUNTRY KITCHEN

LEFT: *A warm chicken pie.*
ABOVE: *The chateau boasts its own chicken coop... strictly eggs only.*

Chicken & leek pie

This is comfort food taken to a new level - a fat, huge, stylish-looking pie that works across both family and formal occasions. Serves 10.

- 2 sheets puff pastry, thawed
- 1 free-range chicken
- 12 chicken wings
- 750 ml white wine
- bouquet garni (see page 59)
- 1 carrot, peeled and chopped
- 3 cloves garlic
- seasoning
- 5 T olive oil
- 600 g leeks, washed and sliced into pennies
- 2 T butter
- 2 T plain flour
- 125 ml full cream
- 3 eggs

Recommended wine: Harvest Moon Sauvignon Blanc

Line a buttered springform pan with one sheet of puff pastry. Prick a few holes in the pastry with a fork. Keep it in the fridge until you need it.

Heat a large casserole, put the chicken and the wings in the pot, and add the wine. While it's coming to a gentle boil, add the bouquet garni, carrot, garlic and some seasoning. Add water to cover and let the chicken simmer until the meat falls off the bones. Remove from the heat. Spoon the chicken out of the casserole and debone. Pour the fabulous stock through a sieve and keep aside.

In the meantime, pour the olive oil into a heated pan, add the leeks and fry them until they are soft and glossy. Take a medium casserole, melt the butter and stir in the flour with one hand while adding the chicken stock with the other. Fun! Keep adding the stock until you have a thick sauce with a creamy consistency. Remove from the heat. Add the cream. Whisk the eggs and fold them into the sauce. Finally, add the leeks and mix well.

Fold in the chicken, and spoon the whole lot into the prepared pastry shell. Cover with the second sheet of pastry, folding gently around the edges and trim where necessary.

Bake this delicious pie for one hour at 180°C/Gas 4. Serve with a green salad.

LEFT: *The tarts are fantastically colourful.*
ABOVE: *Cherries from the market…*
a springtime delight.

Berry tarts with mascarpone

This dessert was born out of sheer desperation when confronted with an almost empty fridge... just a forgotten roll of frozen pastry, and a tub of mascarpone a second away from its sell-by date! The berries were hunted down in the garden... you don't need many. Serves 6.

- 1 roll puff pastry, thawed
- 125 ml castor sugar
- 250 g mascarpone
- vanilla to taste
- berries of choice
- 125 ml double-thick cream

Mould puff pastry into flan ramekins. Fold the castor sugar into the mascarpone. Add the vanilla, and fold a handful of berries - wild strawberries are great! - into the cheese mixture. Put a dollop in each ramekin, and bake at 180°C/Gas 4 for around 20 minutes. Remove. Add some fresh berries, and serve with a scoop of thick cream.

'Without lunch, what will become of love?' LORENZO DI COMO

Spicy caramelised nuts

The best... my mom does them for Christmas Eve to keep the grownups happy until after gift time. It works every year... Makes enough for the family.

- 50 ml olive oil
- 300 g mixed nuts
- 125 g castor sugar
- ¼ t salt
- 5 ml ground cumin seeds
- 5 ml ground coriander seeds
- 5 cardamom pods, shelled and ground

Heat the oil, add the nuts and sprinkle sugar and salt over the mixture. Cook and stir until the sugar has melted and the nuts are golden. Meanwhile, mix the spices in a bowl. As soon as the nuts are ready, scrape them into the spices and toss quickly. Tip out onto a baking tray lined with buttered paper, and using a fork, separate any that stick together. Leave to cool before serving.

Recommended wine: Fleur du Cap Unfiltered Sauvignon Blanc

Red pepper, black olive & anchovy compote

This compote is a great starter and has its origins somewhere in the south of France. I love to serve it with warm, crusty bread and a glass of sauvignon blanc. Makes enough for 8 people.

- 4 red peppers
- 125 ml extra virgin olive oil
- 250 g black depipped olives
- 4 cloves garlic, peeled
- 10 thyme sprigs, chopped
- 20 anchovies
- 8 mint leaves
- 20 g basil leaves
- freshly milled black pepper

Grill the red peppers, turning them regularly, until the skin has blackened. Remove, let cool and skin. Remove the seeds and slice the peppers in thin slices. Try to catch the piquant juices… never rinse the peppers to get rid of the seeds. That's a punishable offence!

Heat the olive oil in a casserole, and stir in the peppers and olives. Add the garlic and thyme, and cook gently over a low heat for 10 minutes to infuse the flavours. Add the anchovies, turn up the heat slightly, and stir until the anchovies have melted away. Remove from the heat. Chop the mint and basil leaves, and add. Season with the black pepper, cool to room temperature and serve immediately.

LEFT: *This tastes as good as it looks.*
Recommended wine: Harvest Moon Sauvignon Blanc

Lamb shanks with pancetta, fennel & risotto

The best lamb shanks ever… If you're in doubt about what to serve, and if you really want to spoil your friends, just DO it! Serves 10 well.

- 2 T goose fat
- 10 lamb shanks, seasoned with salt and pepper
- 2 medium carrots, peeled and chopped
- 1 celery stick, chopped
- 6 cloves garlic
- 250 g pancetta, cut in cubes
- 1 T fennel seeds
- 1 bottle dry white wine
- bouquet garni (see page 59)
- 1 ℓ lamb stock

Recommended wine: Plaisier de Merle Grand Plaisier

Melt the fat in your biggest pot on top of the stove. Brown the shanks. Add the carrot, celery and garlic, and fry quickly. Add the pancetta and fennel seeds. Pour the white wine over the shanks, add the bouquet garni and stock, and simmer gently for about 2 hours, until the shanks are very tender.

Remove the meat from the pot and keep warm. Reduce the remaining stock and season. Serve with a mushroom risotto and baby vegetables.

Risotto with truffle oil

Serves 10, with a little left over for the cook!

- 100 g butter
- 3 leeks, chopped
- 600 g risotto rice
- half bottle dry white wine
- lamb stock from your shank pot (see page 43)
- 250 ml cream
- 100 g Gorgonzola cheese
- seasoning
- parboiled baby carrots and leeks to garnish

Melt the butter and fry the leeks until soft. Add the risotto and fry quickly until all the grains are covered with butter. Add the wine, and stir constantly until the alcohol has evaporated and most of the wine has been absorbed. Ladle some stock out of the lamb shank pot - make sure you pick up some of the pancetta at the same time - and stir until it's absorbed. Stir some more.* Stir. Keep stirring. Add more stock and stir. More stock and stirring is needed until the risotto is nearly ready - it should be slightly al dente. Add cream. Stir it in, and add the Gorgonzola. Stir some more. Add seasoning. Stir until the risotto is beautifully creamy and tasty.

Dish up in huge soup bowls, add a dash of truffle oil, place shank on top, and garnish with parboiled baby carrots and leeks.

* This is absolutely fabulous for upper arms!

Asparagus with salsa verde

Asparagus can be difficult with wine - but this recipe is one of the best chardonnay matches I've ever come across. Serves 4.

- 20 asparagus spears, trimmed and rinsed
- 125 ml extra virgin olive oil
- 20 sprigs flat-leaf parsley
- 2 cloves garlic, peeled and chopped
- 150 ml capers
- juice of half a lemon
- salt and freshly ground black pepper

Steam the asparagus gently in a flat saucepan, and take off the heat while still crunchy. Drain and toss gently with a little of the olive oil. Season lightly.

Put the parsley, garlic, capers, the rest of the olive oil and the lemon juice in a food processor or blender, and chop finely. Transfer to a bowl, season to taste and serve poured over the warm asparagus.* Garnish with a sprig of parsley or even an anchovy!

* Salsa verde can also be served with artichokes that have been quick-boiled in salted water. Remove the leaves and eat the soft, fleshy parts, as well as the heart.

RIGHT: *The neighbour's covetable chimney.*
FAR RIGHT: *Bright-purple artichokes.*
Recommended wine: Plaisier de Merle Chardonnay

Chicken breasts with sauce Albufera

This recipe has done the rounds of a veritable heap of famous chefs - I don't know who to credit. Pass it off as your own! The sauce is also divine with any game birds. I've sometimes used guineafowl breasts, using the carcasses for the original stock. Serves 8.

- 50 ml goose fat or olive oil
- 8 chicken breasts
- sea salt and pepper to taste

For the sauce
- 2 ℓ chicken stock
- 12 chicken wings
- 1 celery stick, sliced
- 3 carrots, peeled and sliced
- 1 leek, trimmed and sliced
- 1 bouquet garni (see page 59)
- 2 bay leaves
- 10 peppercorns
- 25 ml full cream
- 100 g foie gras - if you can't find fresh, a 125 g tin will do. Eat what's left over behind the kitchen door - I do it regularly!

Heat the fat or oil in a flat pan. Fry the chicken breasts quickly on both sides and put on a warm platter to rest. Season to taste and serve with the sauce Albufera on a dollop of crushed potatoes.

SAUCE

Bring the chicken stock to the boil in a big casserole. Add the wings, celery, carrots, leek, bouquet garni, bay leaves and peppercorns, and cook until the meat is almost falling from the bones and all the flavours are fully integrated. If you're tempted to quickly steal and gobble down a wing, do it now… they're delish! Remove the casserole from the heat, pour the contents through a sieve and back into the pot. Let it simmer until the stock has reduced by half. Add the cream and the foie gras. Stir gently until the foie gras has melted into the sauce and the sauce has thickened. Spoon this sublime sauce over the chicken breasts and serve with crushed potatoes.

LEFT: *From left… Blanche, Madeleine, Chique, Noisette and (in the front of the picture) Poulette.*
Recommended wine: Flagstone Two Roads

Roasted peppers with baby tomatoes

If you ever need to cater for a vegan, leave out the anchovies - this is also a fantastic main course. Just don't accompany it with unfiltered wine... Serves 8.

- 4 red peppers
- 75 ml extra virgin olive oil
- 2 leeks, diced and washed
- 6 anchovies
- 20 baby tomatoes
- 250 ml basil leaves, chopped
- 3 cloves garlic, finely chopped
- salt and freshly ground pepper

Preheat the oven to 200°C/Gas 6. Lightly oil a large, shallow baking pan. Halve the red peppers lengthwise and clean out the seeds and pith. Arrange the peppers, open ends up, in the pan. Add 20 ml olive oil to a frying pan, heat it gently and sauté the leeks in the oil until translucent. Add the anchovies and stir the mixture until the anchovies have melted. Remove from the heat. Halve the tomatoes lengthwise and toss in a bowl with the basil and garlic. Fold the leek mixture into the tomato and basil mixture and toss well. Add the rest of the oil, salt and freshly ground black pepper to taste. Divide the mixture among the peppers and roast in the hot oven until the peppers are tender, between 15 and 20 minutes. Serve as a starter with a handful of rocket per plate and a basil leaf for garnish.

For a change - replace the leek and anchovy mixture with a spoonful of tapenade in each pepper - a very zesty taste!

LEFT: *The food of love?*

ABOVE RIGHT: *A little French moment...*

'It's difficult to think anything but pleasant thoughts while eating a homegrown tomato.' LEWIS GRIZZARD

CHAPTER 3

NGELS AND PEACOCKS

Finding a massive - 45 litre - Rosieres-with-a-past iron pot on an antique market, was second only to carrying it over the threshold into the kitchen... shooing the resident peacock out of the way at the same time! And judging by the ensuing mind-blowing ragout of oxtail, tripe and trotters, coq au vin, and all the rest of the stews and cassoulets, yes, size is everything! Once you're the owner of a truly huge family-friendly pot you'll know what I mean.

In front of the kitchen on the chateau grounds is a gentle meadow with knee-high wild flowers one could get lost in. It took me a while to realise that it was here I had to look for the photographer whenever he went missing - I'd find him taking a nap on a lovely old floral rug!

Following the gentle slope up towards the dovecote, nestling in an all-white wild rose garden, waits a small stone angel. In silent memory of all the mothers who have visited La Creuzette. ⚜

LEFT: *An angel for all the mothers who visit La Creuzette.*
FAR LEFT: *This old sundial stands in the middle of the meadow.*

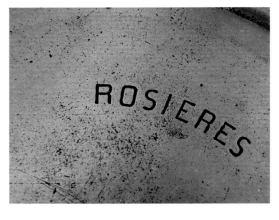

Red peppers with tuna

It seems like an odd combination, but the sweetness of the peppers and the meatiness of the tuna make for a surprisingly satisfying - but light - summer lunch. Serves 6 as a main course.

- 3 red peppers, halved lengthwise and seeded
- 60 ml olive oil
- 250 g fresh tuna fillet
- sea salt and freshly ground black pepper
- zest and juice of 1 lemon
- 1 small green chilli, seeded and chopped
- 1 teaspoon fresh oregano, chopped

Brush the peppers with some of the olive oil and cook under the grill until soft. Set aside. Season tuna and panfry over high heat in olive oil, turning once. Chill and slice into small cubes. Chop zest, set some aside, and mix the rest with the lemon juice, chilli, oregano and the rest of the olive oil. Add the tuna and toss. Fill the pepper halves with the mixture, sprinkle with reserved zest and serve on rocket.

ABOVE FAR LEFT: *The old Rosieres stamp in the lid.*
BELOW FAR LEFT: *I just love using this ancient colander...
for absolutely everything.*
LEFT: *Roasted red peppers just before I peeled them. Slice them
thinly and use in a salad.*

Ragout of oxtail

A huge casserole of oxtail is such a satisfying sight after a long day. This dish loses the normal red wine, which can sometimes make it look quite sludgy. I use white wine instead, and serve it with a rich red! Serves 4.

- 60 g goose fat
- 1 oxtail, about 1,2 kg, cut up
- 2 large carrots, peeled and chopped
- 1 onion, peeled and chopped; or 4 leeks, sliced and rinsed
- 50 g flour
- 1 bottle dry white wine
- chicken stock to cover
- bouquet garni (see page 59)
- seasoning
- 16 preserved chestnuts (optional)*

Recommended wine: La Cave Cabernet Sauvignon

Heat the fat in a large casserole, and brown the oxtail pieces. Add the carrots and leeks or onion, brown, and sprinkle with the flour. Stir the mixture and fry it a little more before you add the wine. Empty the bottle of wine into the pot and bring to a fast boil before topping up with the chicken stock. Drop in the bouquet garni. Simmer gently for about 3 hours - the meat should almost be coming off the bone and the liquid would have reduced to a delicious thick, glossy sauce. Season with salt and pepper.

Remember to remove the bouquet garni before serving the oxtail.

To create a thoroughly French dish, add the chestnuts to the cooked oxtail and warm gently. Serve with couscous and Provençal vegetables.

* These are readily available at good delis.

LEFT: *Heavenly!*
ABOVE: *No chateau is allowed to be*
without a peacock.
ABOVE RIGHT: *The dovecote next to the*
rose garden.

Tiramisu with melted white chocolate

To add more decadence to an already seriously rich dessert, I thought this idea of adding a soupçon of white, creamy chocolate sauce was stunning! Serves 6.

- 600 g good quality white chocolate
- 2 eggs, separated
- 75 g castor sugar
- 100 ml espresso coffee
- 25 ml cognac
- 30 savioardi biscuits (finger biscuits)
- 250 g mascarpone
- 125 ml fresh cream

Roughly grate 200 g of the white chocolate. Beat the egg yolks with the castor sugar until frothy. Beat the egg whites until soft peaks form, and fold into the mixture. Pour the espresso and cognac into a flat dish and gently dip one side of each biscuit quickly in the brandied coffee.

Layer the biscuits alternatively with the layers of mascarpone and grated chocolate. You can do this in individual ramekins or one large glass bowl.

Meanwhile, gently melt the rest of the chocolate in a double boiler. Fold the cream into the chocolate to form a lovely white chocolate sauce.

Serve the tiramisu with a spoonful of sauce dribbled over or around it. Yum...

'Happiness: a good bank account, a good cook and a good digestion.' JEAN JACQUES ROUSSEAU

ANGELS AND PEACOCKS

Bouquet garni

I find great pleasure in making my own bouquet garni... starting with a stroll through the herb garden collecting the ingredients.

- 1 leek
- 1 sprig oregano
- 5 sprigs rosemary
- 1 thin celery stick, 8 cm long
- 2 bay leaves
- 1 piece string, 12 cm long

Trim the bottom of the leek and remove the two outer leaves by cutting them lengthwise. Rinse well. Fold all the herbs, including the celery, into the first leek leaf. Fold the second one over the open end of the first. Fold the 2 bay leaves around the 'parcel' and tie with the piece of string. Add the bouquet garni to any pot au feu or daube and taste the difference!

FAR LEFT: *The entrance to the vegetable and herb garden at Chateau la Creuzette.*
LEFT: *A perfect bouquet garni.*
ABOVE RIGHT: *All the various elements...*

Pheasant & chestnut soup

For all the hunters out there. On occasion I've used guineafowl instead of pheasant... it's superb. Serves 6.

For the stock
- 100 ml extra virgin olive oil
- 2 pheasants, ready for the pot
- 3 leeks, washed and chopped
- 1 large carrot, peeled and chopped roughly
- 4 cloves garlic, peeled and chopped
- 2 ℓ chicken stock
- 1 bouquet garni (see page 59)
- seasoning

For the soup
- 4 pheasant legs and 4 thighs, from the stock you've made
- 50 ml olive oil
- 150 g peeled and diced mixed turnips, carrots and sweet potatoes
- 1,5 ℓ pheasant stock
- 250 g tinned or bottled chestnuts, cut in quarters

STOCK

Heat the olive oil in a flameproof stockpot and lightly brown the pheasant carcasses. Add the vegetables to the pot, and sauté until softened. Add the stock and bouquet garni, and bring to the boil. Keep an eye on the pot, and skim the stock regularly to remove any scummy foam. After about an hour, when the meat starts coming off the bone, remove the carcasses and strain the stock through a sieve. Keep the legs and thighs to use in the soup.

SOUP

Debone the pheasant legs and thighs and shred the meat. Heat the olive oil in a saucepan and lightly stir the vegetables in the oil. Pour the stock over and bring to the boil. Simmer for about 15 minutes, until vegetables are soft. Add the shredded meat and the chestnuts to the soup. Season, and spoon into large bowls, distributing the vegetables, meat and chestnuts evenly. Serve with a dollop of aïoli in each bowl (see page 130)... and lots of black pepper.

LEFT: *The chestnuts add a gentle sweetness to this meaty soup.*
ABOVE RIGHT: *In the herb garden...*
Recommended wine: Harvest Moon Shiraz

Tripe & trotters with white wine

I've travelled miles for a bowlful of tripe. After a couple of years of serious tripe hunting, though, I realised it would probably be more economical to just do my own... This is good. Serves 8.

- 150 ml duck fat
- 2 whole sheep tripe, cleaned
- 8 trotters, cleaned
- 750 ml good quality white wine
- 500 ml chicken stock
- 2 carrots, peeled and sliced
- 3 leeks, peeled and sliced
- 6 cloves garlic, peeled
- 1 whole celery stick, rinsed and sliced
- 1 bouquet garni with fresh sage leaves added (see page 59)

LEFT: *This is truly heartwarming. My best.*
Recommended wine: Meerlust Pinot Noir

Heat the fat in a large casserole, and fry the tripe lightly for about 3 minutes... it's all about getting the rich flavour of the duck fat incorporated. Add the trotters, then the wine, and bring to the boil before pouring in the chicken stock. Add the carrots, leeks, garlic, celery and bouquet garni. Bring to a slow simmer and keep it simmering for about 2 hours. Add more liquid if necessary.

When the tripe is soft, remove from the casserole and cut with a pair of scissors into small, bite-sized pieces. Return to the pot. Remove the trotters from the casserole, debone and shred the meat. Return the meat to the casserole. Reduce the liquid to a lovely, thick sauce before you serve the tripe on basmati rice, with a dollop of aïoli or basil pesto (see page 130). Garnish with persillade.

'Wooden spoons are friendly things . . .' MARTIN VERSFELD

Warm rhubarb

Every time I cook rhubarb I am reminded of what Pam Fisher said: just keep it simple. Most of our grandparents grew up with rhubarb, and I think it's high time it was restored to its rightful place, after dinner, as a divine dessert. I sometimes spoon a little cooked rhubarb into ramekins as a sharp little reminder of tastes past, before adding the rest of the ingredients for a crème brulée. Fantastic! Serves 6.

- 1 bunch rhubarb
- 125 ml castor sugar
- 100 ml fruity white wine
- 125 ml thick cream or yoghurt

Cut off the rhubarb leaves and wash the stems. Cut the stems in 8 cm lengths. Dissolve the sugar in the wine and an equal quantity of water, and cook the rhubarb until it is soft. Remove the rhubarb from the pot and reduce the liquid until it becomes syrupy. Reheat the rhubarb in the syrup and serve warm with a scoop of thick cream or yoghurt.

Potato & leek soup

When served cold, this soup is better known as vichyssoise. It was first made in America by a French chef who hailed from Vichy in the Auvergne. Serves 6.

- 6 leeks, green leaves discarded
- 60 g salted butter
- 6-8 potatoes, peeled and chopped roughly
- 1½ ℓ chicken stock
- 250 ml double cream
- salt and freshly ground black pepper to taste
- olive oil and sprigs fresh thyme to garnish

First slice the leeks in thin rounds before rinsing them thoroughly. Heat the butter in a heavy-based saucepan and fry the leeks until softened. Add the potatoes and chicken stock and bring to the boil. Add some water if you think it is necessary. Reduce the heat and let it simmer until the potatoes are soft. Liquidise the soup until it is smooth and creamy, return to the saucepan and reheat gently, adding the cream. Season to taste and serve garnished with a dribble of olive oil and a sprig of thyme.

Recommended wine: Dominion Sugar Bush Ridge Sauvignon Blanc

Coq au vin

Serve in a soup plate on top of a dinner plate, with a chunk of fresh, crusty bread for mopping up the sauces, and baby green beans on the side. Serves 4.

- 500 g bacon, chopped
- olive oil
- 1,2 kg jointed chicken or, if available, 2 poussin, halved
- 2 onions, sliced and chopped
- 2 peeled carrots, chopped
- 4 cloves garlic, crushed
- 2 huge marrow bones (beef)
- large bouquet garni (see page 59)
- 4 bay leaves
- 1 t thyme
- freshly ground black pepper
- 30 g flour
- 2 bottles red wine
- 1 ℓ chicken stock

- 20 small onions
- 500g mushrooms
- 50 ml butter
- 25 g sugar
- 2 T brandy

Braise the bacon in some olive oil until the fat runs. Remove. Brown the chicken in the same oil. Add the onions, carrots, garlic, marrow bones, bouquet garni and herbs. Sprinkle with black pepper and flour and stir these in before adding the wine and stock. Cook at a slow simmer for about 45 minutes until the chicken is tender.

In the meantime, boil the onions until they're just soft.

A few minutes before you're ready to serve, brown the mushrooms in olive oil and add to the casserole. Caramelise the onions in butter and sugar, and add. Flambé the brandy - it's easiest to do this if you warm it in a small pan over a low flame first - and pour it over the chicken. Serve in soup plates with crusty bread on the side.

Recommended wine: Fleur du Cap Unfiltered Merlot

CHAPTER 4

 ILLAGE LIFE

Charroux village could also be called the Village of Three Hundred Wells, most of which are to be found inside the mostly medieval houses. If you take into account that there are only 320 inhabitants in the village, this begins to explain the uniqueness of this heartbreakingly beautiful little place.

During Roman times the fortified village of Charroux was known as Quadrivium. The village survived the Plague (1347 to 1352) and the Hundred Year War (which ended in 1453) reasonably well - two of the huge stone Roman gates, as well as the original cobbles of the streets, still exist. Even the medieval street names such as Rue de la Poulaillerie (chicken farmer) and Rue de la Ferraillerie (ironmonger) are still in use.

The village is officially categorised as One of the Most Beautiful Villages of France and lies in the heart of the Bourbonais, not too far from Vichy. From the lookout point at the Belvedere, you can look into eternity... or Bellenaves, where the weekly fresh produce market is held! On the far horizon you'll also see the volcanos of the Auvergne, which provided the cobbles for most of the roads.

Living in Charroux has its own charms, one of which is having the most amazing mustard and walnut oil shop as a neighbour. Waking up with the smell of crushed walnuts does tend to get your appetite going… The mustard, known as Moutarde de Charroux, is made with the wines from St Pourcain, the oldest vineyard in France.

And then of course there is the soap maker in his tower, the medieval clock collector, the spring water that pours from the taps in your home, and the fact that as soon as the last fresh bread at the boulangerie is sold, it closes for the day… C'est la vie! ⚜

ABOVE RIGHT: *Foie gras with Sauternes jelly is truly decadent.*
ABOVE MIDDLE AND LEFT: *Small details make this village special.*

Foie gras with Sauternes jelly

Start this the day before. The golden jelly looks like jewels on the plate - a very celebratory starter.
Serves 12 generous portions.

For the jelly

- 1 bottle Sauternes (a sweet white wine)
- 250 ml castor sugar
- 5 leaves gelatine

For the foie gras

- 1 whole raw goose liver (about 550 g)
- 200 ml cognac
- sea salt and freshly ground black pepper to taste
- brioche, to serve

Recommended wine: Groot Constantia Grand Constance

JELLY

Heat the Sauternes in a deep saucepan, and stir the sugar into the wine. Add the gelatine leaves and gently stir until melted. Pour the liquid into a flat container and place it in the refrigerator.

FOIE GRAS

Heat the oven to 180°C/Gas 4. Clean the foie gras properly, removing all veins and sinews. Make a bowl out of a piece of aluminium foil, place the foie gras in it, pour over the cognac, season and wrap carefully. Bake for 9 minutes. Turn the heat off and leave the foie gras to cool in the oven. Once it's completely cool, remove from the oven and refrigerate overnight.

Before serving, gently break the foie gras out of the fat mould that will have formed around it. Melt this fat in a frying pan, slice the foie gras into serving portions, and quick-fry it in the cognac-flavoured fat.

Remove the jelly from the refrigerator and cut it in a criss-cross manner with a sharp knife. Spoon the little blocks of golden jelly around a slice of toasted brioche, slide a slice of foie gras on top of the brioche, and garnish with a sprig of thyme.

Panfried fillet with mushrooms

This is one of those fabulously easy and truly foolproof recipes. The girls' way of doing a great fillet... no smelly fires and certainly no ash over your cashmere! Serves 10 generously.

- 1 whole fillet
- 25 ml olive oil
- butter
- 1 punnet small mushrooms, fried
- 125 ml fresh cream

Heat a large pan and melt a dollop of butter in it. Add the olive oil and wait until it gives off a little smoke. Add the fillet and seal quickly. Turn the heat down a little and let it cook in its own juices, turning regularly, until done. Add the mushrooms and cream. Serve with baby potatoes and lightly caramelised tomatoes.

RIGHT: *Stone flowerpots are all over the village.*
FAR RIGHT: *A festive sweep of red.*
Recommended wine: Allesverloren Cabernet Sauvignon

Vegetables with persillade

The quantities in this wonderful dish depend entirely on your own whim. And it looks beautiful on a huge platter.

- baby artichokes
- little onions, peeled and parboiled in salted water
- unpeeled garlic cloves
- bouquet garni (see page 59)
- 100 ml butter, salted
- chiffonade of lettuce - cut up 'kerk-basaar' style in thin strips

FAR LEFT: *A pastoral scene next to the road.*
ABOVE RIGHT: *The back road out of the village.*
MIDDLE AND BELOW RIGHT: *Sweeping views from Charroux.*

Heat oven to 180°C/Gas 4. Put the artichokes, onions, garlic and bouquet garni into an oven dish, and cover with a lid or a sheet of foil. Sweat for about 30 minutes and remove from the oven. In the meantime, heat some butter in a pan and add the chiffonade of lettuce to the butter. Give it a quick swirl before adding it, with the butter, to the vegetables. Just before serving you can add any of the following vegetables to the dish: diced little green beans, lightly braised; broccoli florets, parboiled; small courgettes, julienned and sautéed; or raw peas

Vegetables that have been sweated in butter can be finished by swirling in a little double cream, off the heat. Serve this scattered with a persillade - mix together a bunch of flat-leaf parsley, roughly chopped, and zest of 2 lemons.

Pears in red wine & honey

My mom's recipe for red wine pears was the one most of us grew up with... a winter wine sauce smelling of cinnamon and cloves. Recently I saw a recipe for red fruit with honey and brown sugar and... voila! Serves 6.

- 6 firm pears
- 750 ml fruity red wine
- 100 ml honey
- 100 g brown sugar
- vanilla to taste... I like to use vanilla paste or vanilla bean, scraped

Peel the pears, leaving the stalk intact. Combine the wine, honey, brown sugar and vanilla in a large pot. Bring to the boil and simmer until the sugar has dissolved. Add the pears, placing them upright. Poach slowly until tender, about 15 minutes. Remove from the heat. Reduce the wonderful wine sauce until it has a syrupy consistency. Serve each pear with a spoonful of syrup dribbled over and a scoop of crème fraîche.

FAR LEFT: *Detail of a window in the village church.*
LEFT: *Ancient road sign showing a crossroad outside Charroux.*

Marinated olives with bay leaves

This looks lovely and should be served at an alfresco lunch or picnic.

- 100 ml extra virgin olive oil
- 6 anchovies
- 50 g slightly marinated olives... black or green
- 6 cinnamon sticks
- 6 bay leaves, dried or fresh

Heat the olive oil in a saucepan and melt the anchovies in the oil, constantly stirring. Add the olives and toss quickly. Add the cinnamon sticks and bay leaves after you have removed the pan from the heat. Serve the olives in separate bowls, making sure that each bowl has its share of cinnamon sticks and bay leaves.

RIGHT: *Chef off her feet.*
FAR RIGHT: *The chef's tools.*

ABOVE: *Enjoy a pastis at the local café whilst you wait for the Mme from the moutardier to open her shop after the lunch hour.*

Caprese salad

This is a classic recipe - I'm serving it in a fresh way, which really highlights the way it works. Use the best olive oil you can find. Serves 4.

- 2 ripe tomatoes, each sliced into 6 rounds
- sea salt and freshly ground black pepper
- 1 round of buffalo mozzarella, sliced... cut the edges off, sprinkle some salt and olive oil on them and eat quickly when no-one's looking
- freshly chopped basil
- 100 ml extra virgin olive oil

Salt the tomato slices individually. Salt and pepper the mozzarella slices, and let them rest.

Take 4 plates and place 3 tomato slices on each. Sprinkle the basil over the tomatoes. Place the mozzarella slices in a little stack next to the tomatoes. Pour 25 ml olive oil in each of 4 tot glasses and put a glass on each plate, next to the cheese. Serve with crusty white bread.

ABOVE RIGHT: *The entire village of Charroux is drenched in roses during the summer months.*
BELOW RIGHT: *Flower boxes abound.*

BELOW: *Quails and artichokes at the market.*

Deboned, stuffed quail

Years ago, I was asked to cater for the opening of a Stellenbosch Cap Classique cellar. Chèvre being an excellent partner to bubbles, I prepared these. Serves 6.

- 50 ml extra virgin olive oil
- 300 g artichoke hearts, sliced
- 150 g green olives, depipped and sliced
- 2 sundried peppadews, sliced
- 3 cloves garlic, chopped
- 50 g chives, chopped
- 125 g cashew nuts, grilled
- 250 g chèvre, sliced
- 6 quails, deboned
- sea salt
- freshly ground black pepper

Heat the olive oil in a pot and add the artichokes, olives, peppadews, garlic, chives and cashew nuts. Mix over the heat, remove from the stove and fold the cheese into the mixture.

Using a tablespoon, fill the cavity of each quail with the stuffing, and place the quails, legs and wingtips up, on a baking tray. Smear them with the remnants of the oil in the pot. Season and bake at 180°C/Gas 4 for around 35 minutes, or until the juices run clear when pricked with a sharp knife. Serve the quails with polenta or couscous, and a helping of baby green beans with garlic butter.

ABOVE: *Ancient walnut press still in use.*
Recommended wine: Rust En Vrede Shiraz

BELOW: *Ancient window and flowerpot.*

Crème brulée with burnt honey

The idea for this dessert was shamelessly stolen from a magazine cover I once saw. I've never seen anything more simple or more pretty! I started to demonstrate it during cooking classes in Cape Town and France... and it turned out to be a favourite. I normally bake this in a heat-resistant glass. Serves 6.

- 350 ml cream
- 175 ml honey
- 2 eggs, plus two extra yolks, whisked

Pour cream into a pot, add 50 ml honey and heat until steaming. Do not boil. Let it cool down and whisk into the egg mixture. Pour into ovenproof ramekins and bake in a bain-marie for about 30 minutes at 180°C/Gas 4. Bring the rest of the honey to the boil with 50 ml water, and pour on top of the cooked custards. Serve immediately.

Carpaccio of beef or venison

Anyone who has a hunter in the family needs to know about this one. It's a wow, and it's instant!
Serves 6 as a starter portion.

- 325 ml extra virgin olive oil

- 5 ml coriander seeds

- 5 ml paprika

- 5 ml dried sage

- 2,5 ml sea salt

- freshly ground black pepper

- 1 fillet of beef or venison (about 300 g
  from the chunkiest bit of the fillet)

- 50 ml capers, chopped

- 150 g Parmesan, grated

- rocket

Heat 125 ml olive oil in a saucepan and lightly fry the coriander, paprika, sage, salt and pepper. Add the fillet to the pan and quickly seal on all sides. Remove the meat to a sheet of plastic wrap, pour over most of the frying liquid, and wrap lightly. Freeze until needed. Since the meat needs to defrost a little, remove the fillet from the freezer 20 minutes before you plan to slice the meat. Drizzle a serving platter with olive oil. Slice the fillet extremely thinly, placing each slice onto the serving platter. After each layer, season the meat, sprinkle capers and Parmesan over, and pour on more olive oil. Repeat until all the meat has been layered onto the platter. You can also do individual servings. Serve with a handful of fresh, green rocket per person. Lovely!

LEFT: *Charolais cattle in a field close to Charroux.*
Recommended wine: Rust En Vrede Shiraz

'First, catch your hare...'

HANNAH GLASSE

LEFT: *All the ingredients for a sumptuous rabbit stew, ready for the pot.*

Rabbit in red wine with chestnuts

Rabbits can be found at any specialist butcher. Chestnuts - well, I prefer fresh, but the tinned version works beautifully, and those are widely available at delis throughout the country. This is a fabulous wintry dish to serve with a hearty red or two. Serves 8.

- 50 ml olive oil
- 6 leeks, sliced into pennies and washed
- 500 g pork belly, cut into thin slices
- 2 carrots, peeled and chopped roughly
- 2 rabbits, cut into six pieces each
- 750 ml red wine
- 750 ml chicken stock
- 1 bouquet garni with lots of sage (see page 59)
- 2 cloves garlic, chopped
- 25 ml black pepper, freshly ground
- 500 g chestnuts
- sea salt and milled black pepper

Heat the olive oil in a heavy-bottomed pot and sauté the leeks. Add the pork belly and fry until browned. Add the carrots and then the rabbit. Brown the meat properly before adding the wine. Let it simmer until the alcohol has evaporated... you will smell when it's gone! Add the stock, bouquet garni, garlic and pepper. Simmer until the meat is done, about 1½ hours. Remove the rabbit from the pot, reduce the lovely stock until it has a thick, glossy consistency - then add the chestnuts. Taste the sauce and, if necessary, add some salt. Then gently reintroduce the rabbit pieces to the pot to reheat. Serve immediately with small white potatoes Lyonnaise (see page 91).

ABOVE RIGHT: *The tree-lined road to Gannat.*
Recommended wine: La Cave Merlot

Potatoes Lyonnaise

This is equally good served with rabbit in red wine or ragout of oxtail.

- 24 small white potatoes
- 100 ml duck or goose fat
- salt and pepper
- 100 ml flat-leaf parsley, chopped

Boil the potatoes in their skins until they are almost cooked through. Drain, let them cool a little, and peel. In the meantime, heat the fat in a casserole. When it is nice and hot, add the potatoes and cook, turning them constantly, until tender. Remove from the fat, drain slightly, and toss gently with the parsley. Season and serve with the rabbit (see page 89) spooned on top in huge steamy heaps... yum!

'My favourite animal is a steak.' FRAN LEBOWITZ

ABOVE RIGHT: *Herbs at the nursery.*
BOTTOM RIGHT: *Wheat field with silo, just outside the village.*

RIGHT: *Rue de la Poulaillerie, a medieval road that originates from the Roman times.*

CHAPTER 5

HE WEDNESDAY MARKET

In the quaint village of Bellenaves, within easy Vespa distance of Charroux, Wednesday is market day.* I normally start my shopping with serious concentration at the fish stall, where a half dozen of the most delectable, fat oysters from the Brittany coast are lovingly shucked by the monger… and with equal care, devoured by me! A fabulous start to some serious shopping.

From here, into my basket go thick white asparagus, oranges and limes, sweet potatoes, Puy lentils, artichokes and garlic, fresh bunches of rosemary and thyme… At the cheese stand you're spoiled for choice, with ash-rolled chèvre, Soumaintrain, sublime Brie and Camembert, Reblochon, Roquefort, St Nectaire, Comte and one of the oldest cheeses in France, Cantal.

If you happen to be in the Auvergne during autumn, you will also be enchanted by the array of wild mushrooms available… cep, specifically tête de nègre or the Moor's head, chanterelle, morel, horn of plenty and even, on a good day, a black truffle or two.

LEFT: *'To market, to market!'… The abundance of produce blows your mind.*

From the butcher I get queue de boeuf or oxtail, and a succulent rack of lamb. And on the way home I stop next to the little winding road en route to Charroux to pick some blackberries for dessert. ⚜

The other market days in villages that are very close to Charroux are on Saturday in Gannat and on Sunday in Chantelle.

White asparagus & fried sage leaves

I serve this as a starter with a glass of cold chardonnay. White asparagus is only available for a short period every season, and it's so delicious that, frankly, I can't get enough! It looks very elegant with the dusty colour of the fried sage.

- 5 asparagus spears per person, cleaned and trimmed
- 250 ml good quality olive oil
- handful sage leaves
- seasoning

Pour a little water into a frying pan. Bring to a gentle boil, add a little salt and the asparagus, and cook until you can slip a sharp knife into the thickest part of the stem. The asparagus must be cooked but still crunchy. Divide among individual plates.

Heat the olive oil in a small saucepan until really hot, remove from the heat and add the sage leaves. Let it stand while the leaves crisp, then spoon over the plated asparagus. Season to taste and serve.

RIGHT: *Deliciously sweet baby onions to add to your basket.*
Recommended wine: Uitkyk Chardonnay

LEFT: *Lamb and rosemary in a copper pan. What a delight!*

Rack of lamb with fresh rosemary & olive oil

This falls into the 'favorite food' category. It's a quick meal that can hold its own in any conversation.

- 2 lamb chops per person
- 20 sprigs rosemary
- 100 ml extra virgin olive oil
- sea salt and freshly ground black pepper

Smear a roasting pan with olive oil, and line with all the rosemary sprigs. Layer the lamb chops onto the rosemary, season, and dribble with the rest of the olive oil. Place under a hot grill until chops have browned. Turn over and repeat. Serve immediately with a salad of asparagus, green beans and basil or sage. Don't hesitate to add a couple of boiled-in-the-skin baby potatoes. Fab!

Recommended wine: Rust En Vrede Estate

'As life is an art in France,
so woman is an artist.'

EDITH WHARTON

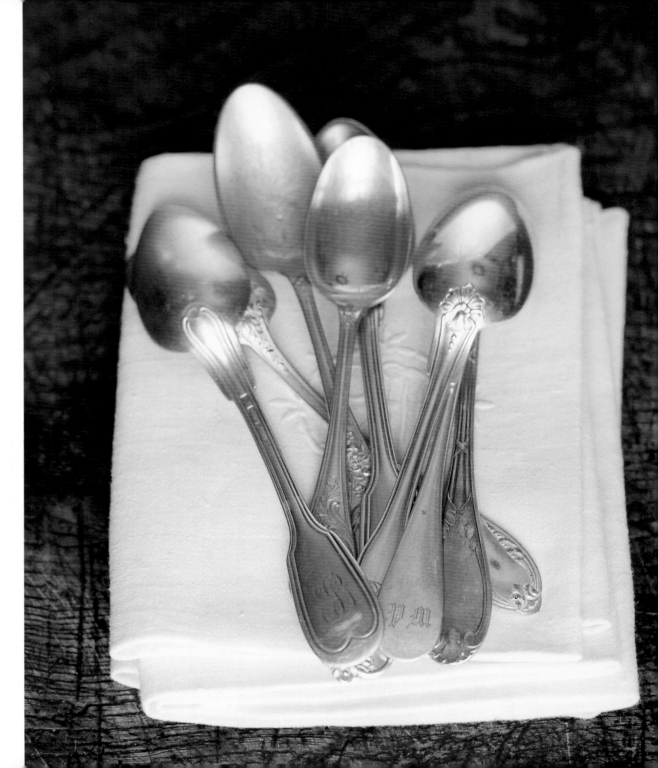

Creamy sweet potato & thyme soup

This is a truly creamy, comforting soup. The combined flavour of the sweet potato and thyme is hugely satisfying. Real fireplace food. Serves 8.

- 50 ml extra virgin olive oil
- 5 cloves garlic, peeled and sliced
- 1 large onion, diced
- 1 celery stick, diced
- 1 red chilli, diced
- 1 kg sweet potatoes, peeled and diced
- 6 sprigs thyme
- 1 ℓ chicken stock
- 150 ml double cream
- seasoning
- extra cream and thyme for garnishing

Gently heat the olive oil in a flameproof saucepan. Fry the garlic lightly until it becomes a light caramel colour. Add the onion, celery and chilli and fry until soft. Add the sweet potatoes and keep tossing until all the pieces are coated with the oil and onion mixture. Add the thyme and stock and simmer for about 20 minutes or until soft.

Remove the thyme, purée the soup in a liquidiser and return to the saucepan. Reheat, stir in the cream, season and serve immediately. Garnish with a dollop of cream and a sprig of thyme. Lovely!

Orange cake with lime mascarpone

This is an excellent cake. I serve it in winter with a glass of Sauternes - or any of our local botrytis wines.
Makes 2 x 20 cm cakes, and serves 16 with plenty left over for you. Keeps well in a sealed container.

- 2 large oranges
- 6 eggs
- 550 g sugar
- 1 t baking powder
- 550 g ground almonds
- 10 g cinnamon
- zest and juice of 2 limes
- 250 g mascarpone cheese

LEFT: *Orange cake nicely tucked under a glass antique market find.*

Place the oranges whole into a saucepan with enough water to cover. Simmer for an hour or until the oranges are completely tender. Change the simmering water up to three times to get rid of any traces of bitterness. Cut the oranges in half, remove the seeds, and purée the flesh and peels in a blender.

Preheat the oven to 180°C/Gas 4.

Butter and flour 2 x 20 cm springform tins, and line the bottoms with baking paper. Beat the eggs and 500 g of the sugar until pale and thick. Combine the baking powder, ground almonds and cinnamon, and stir in. Fold into the orange purée. Pour into the prepared tins and bake on the centre shelf for 60 minutes, or until a skewer inserted into the centre of the cake comes out clean. Turn the cakes out onto a cake rack.

While they're cooling, make the lime mascarpone: combine the rest of the sugar with the lime zest, juice and mascarpone. Adjust the lime juice and sugar if necessary.

Serve the cake in wedges with a spoonful of lime mascarpone and some mixed berries.

FRENCH CHEESES INCLUDE ALL THE MAIN MILK STYLES:

Chèvre (goat), vache (cow), brebis (sheep) or melange (blended)... French cheeses are extraordinary. They vary in consistency from soft to tender or semi-hard; in flavour from mild to strong; and for the discerning, from pasteurised to raw milk. Raw milk is the more sought-after because of a stronger, more robust flavour.

Happy cheese tasting!

Fromage de chèvre on toast with salad

This is fast becoming a must-do for all cooks - and a must-order when you see it on a menu! I would on occasion pour a little olive oil in a small pan and quick-fry some baby tomatoes in the oil before serving them with the salad greens. It's lovely. Serves 6.

- 6 slices fresh rye bread
- 6 T olive oil
- 125 g basil pesto
- 6 slices goats' cheese
- soft green salad leaves, mixed with small tomatoes
- 6 T walnut oil

Place the bread on a pan, and spoon the olive oil over. Drop a dollop of pesto on each slice before adding the cheese. Quick-grill the bread and cheese. Toss the leaves and tomatoes with walnut oil, place the slices on top, and serve.

Recommended wine: Uitkyk Sauvignon Blanc

Osso bucco

A centuries-old recipe from Milan; and very far removed from the tomato-style veal shank that we all know. This is a simple and lovely meal that is especially good on a cold night. Serves 6.

- 12 pieces veal shank, 4 cm thick
- plain flour, seasoned
- 60 ml olive oil
- 60 g butter
- garlic to taste
- 250 ml dry white wine
- 1 bay leaf
- pinch allspice
- pinch cinnamon

For the gremolata
- 2 lemons
- 1 large bunch fresh parsley
- 10 cloves garlic, peeled

Recommended wine: Flagstone The Music Room

Dust the shanks with seasoned flour. Heat the oil, butter and garlic in a large, heavy saucepan. Add the shanks and cook for about 15 minutes, until well browned. Stand the shanks on their sides in a single layer, pour in the wine and add the bay leaf, allspice and cinnamon. Cover. Cook at low simmer for 15 minutes, then add 125 ml warm water. Continue cooking, covered, for about an hour until the meat is very tender. Add more water if needed. Transfer veal to warm platter and serve with gremolata.

GREMOLATA

Zest the lemons and finely chop the parsley. Crush and chop the garlic cloves. Toss together and sprinkle over the osso bucco just before serving.

'Great food begins with great ingredients.'

LIAM TOMLIN, *SEASON TO TASTE*

'One cannot fix one's eyes on the

commonest

natural production

without finding

food for a

rambling fancy.'

JANE AUSTEN, *MANSFIELD PARK*

Molten chocolate puddings with a white centre

This is, by now, a classic dessert. It originated, as far as I know, with the Roux brothers. To add some zing, I've come up with the idea of placing a small block of soft-centered white Lindt chocolate into the middle of each mould before baking the puddings. The result is spectacular! Start the day before. Serves 8.

- 5 eggs, plus 5 extra yolks
- 125 g unrefined castor sugar
- 250 g bitter, dark (at least 70% cocoa) chocolate, broken up
- 250 g unsalted butter
- 50 g plain flour, sifted
- 8 blocks soft-centered white chocolate

In a bowl, beat together the eggs, yolks and sugar until pale. Meanwhile, melt the chocolate and butter gently in a bowl set over a pan of hot water. Remove from the heat. Slowly add to the egg mixture, beating until smooth. Fold in the flour. Pour into buttered moulds before the mixture begins to firm up. Put a block of white chocolate into the middle of each. Chill overnight.

The next day, heat the oven to 180°C/Gas 4. Bake for about 10-15 minutes, until the centres 'puff' and look dry. Turn out and serve.

Bagna cauda

This is an easy recipe for a delicious dip.
Long summer afternoons come to mind...

- 150 ml extra virgin olive oil
- 5 cloves garlic, chopped
- 12 anchovies, drained
- 100 g unsalted butter (optional)

Put the oil in a pan with the garlic and anchovies and cook over a low heat until the anchovies have melted. Remove from the heat and whisk a couple of times. Taste. If you want it to be more creamy, add the butter and whisk. Use this sauce while it's still warm. Serve with vegetables cut up for dipping, such as raw carrots, red peppers, celery, radishes, small tomatoes, artichokes and courgettes.

'Oeuf d'une heure; pain d'un jour; vin d'un an...'
SCHOTT'S FOOD AND DRINK MISCELLANY

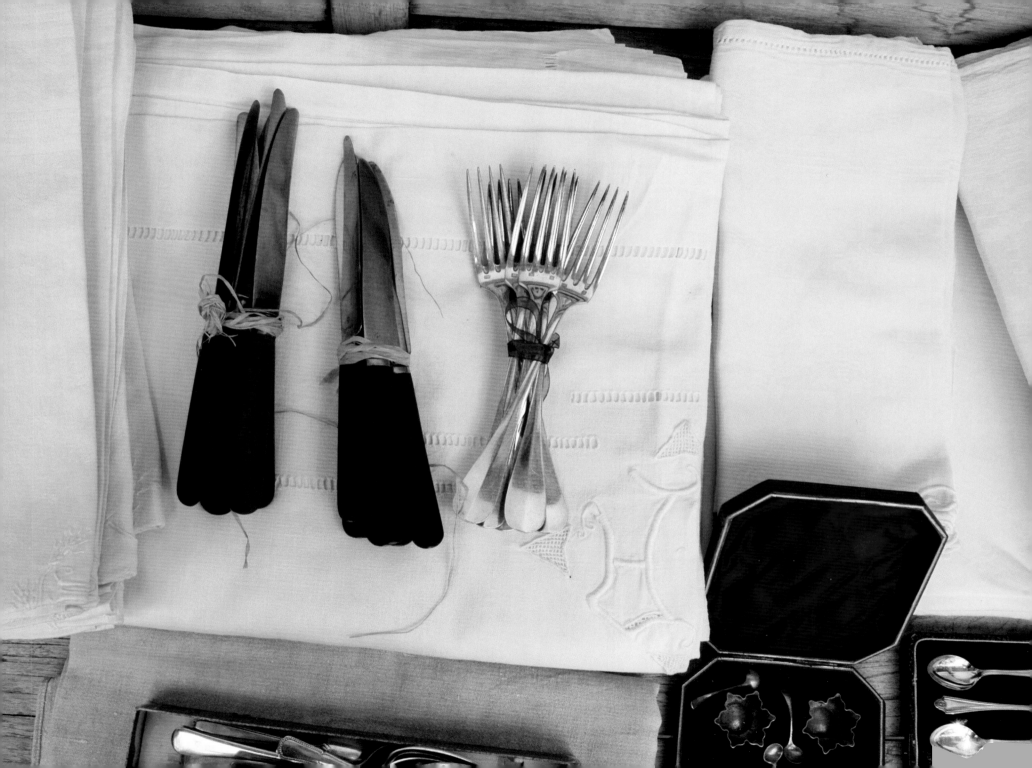

CHAPTER 6

ROCANTE ON A SUNDAY

Part of the Sunday routine is to have a quick croissant with your coffee, and then it's off to the brocante, or antique market. Rows and rows of tables and stalls lining blocked-off streets and squares in tiny villages scattered through the French countryside... nothing can prepare you! You'll find Christofle silver, antique French bed linen, art nouveau and art deco objects, embroidered napkins large enough to cover a small table, huge armoires, stone basins and fireplaces, ancient pewterware, cutlery, copper pots and pans, Limoges porcelain, Laguiole knives, crystal chandeliers... the bounty is endless.

Of all these wonderful Sunday markets, the one nobody wants to miss is on the last Sunday of April in Charroux when the entire fortified village is turned into a market. The antique dealers come from far and wide both to buy and sell. The art lies in being at the market really early, and throwing an expert eye over the stalls before pouncing... and bargaining! What a satisfying pleasure to have a 'brocante' lunch with your entire stash around your tired feet and a glass of red wine from St Pourcain in your hand. Perfect joie de vivre! ⚜

BELOW: *One can find the most amazing collections at Sunday brocantes.*

Tapenade & anchovy vol-au-vents

This is my 16-year-old son's favourite snack... other people will have it as a starter with a glass of crisp white wine. Serves 8.

Tapenade

- 50 g anchovy fillets
- 250 g olives
- 175 g capers, drained
- 200 ml extra virgin olive oil
- 1 lemon, juiced
- freshly ground black pepper

Vol-au-vents

- 1 roll puff pastry, thawed
- 250 g chèvre, cut in eight slices
- tapenade
- 6 anchovies
- 8 chives
- 1 egg, whisked

TAPENADE

Drain the anchovies and put in a food processor with the olives, capers and olive oil. Blend until smooth. Add lemon juice and pepper to taste.

VOL-AU-VENTS

Roll out the thawed puff pastry, and using a sharp knife, cut into eight squares. Put the squares onto a buttered cookie sheet. Put one slice of chèvre on each square. Follow with a dollop of tapenade and an anchovy each. Using your fingers, mould each square of pastry until it resembles a little closed paper bag. 'Tie' each with a chive. Using a pastry brush, paint each with egg and bake at 220°C/Gas 7 for about 15 minutes or until the pastry has turned crispy. Serve with a handful of rocket each.

Recommended wine: Flat Roof Manor Semillon

Chicken with peaches, honey & parsley

I always buy more juicy yellow cling peaches than necessary for this dish, and stack them up on an old pewter platter... also a 'brocante' find. And it's wonderful to walk home with a basket full of fragrant leeks, garlic, parsley, honey... This will serve 4 or 6, depending on the size of your chickens.

- 100 ml extra virgin olive oil
- 1 chicken, cut up into portions
- 25 ml paprika
- 50 ml flour, seasoned with salt and pepper
- 1 celery stick, chopped
- 6 leeks, chopped
- 3 cloves garlic, chopped
- 250 ml chicken stock
- 250 ml orange juice
- 4 peaches, peeled and sliced
- 50 ml honey
- ½ bunch parsley, chopped

Recommended wine: Fleur du Cap Unfiltered Sauvignon Blanc

Heat the olive oil in a pot, and fry the chicken pieces until brown. Dust with paprika and seasoned flour. Add the celery, leeks and garlic, and fry lightly. Add the liquids and simmer for 35 minutes or until the chicken pieces are soft.

Remove the chicken and reduce the stock until it becomes a thick sauce. Add the peaches and honey, season and serve with rice. Garnish with parsley.

LEFT: *This chair is a charming antique market find from a Sunday brocante in a neighbouring village.*

Bella's cheesecake

Let's just do the crust the usual way, by crunching up a packet of short biscuits and stirring the crumbs into 75 ml of melted, unsalted butter. Line a greased baking tin with the crumb mixture and keep in the refrigerator until you need it. Bella's cheesecake filling is the best that I can remember from my childhood days. Serves 10.

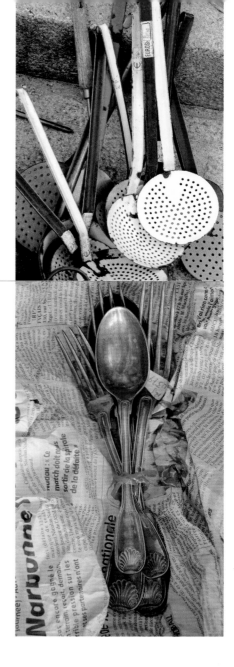

- 3 eggs
- 125 g castor sugar
- 500 ml smooth cream cheese
- 125 ml double cream

Whip the eggs and castor sugar until foamy. Spoon the cream cheese into the mixture and whip thoroughly. Fold in the cream. Pour the mixture into the crust, and bake for 40 minutes in a preheated oven at 160°C/Gas 3. When the cake has risen and set, turn the oven off and open the oven door. Allow the cake to cool down within the oven. Serve in thick slices and burst into song!

'Once a woman has forgiven her man, she must not reheat his sins for breakfast.'

MARLENE DIETRICH

Pasta with red pepper sauce

This is lovely served alongside lightly grilled salmon trout - and, of course, just by itself. Serves 4.

- 2 red peppers, grilled, pitted and peeled
- 125 ml extra virgin olive oil
- 2,5 ml each paprika, cardamom and ginger powder
- 2 cloves garlic, peeled and chopped
- 4 servings tagliolini
- 50 ml extra virgin olive oil
- 5 ml sea salt
- black pepper to taste

Slice the peppers roughly and place in a blender. Heat the olive oil gently in a frying pan, and lightly fry the spices and garlic. Add the mix to the peppers in the blender. Purée. Return to the pan and reheat without bringing to a boil. Season with sea salt and freshly ground black pepper.

Meanwhile, cook the tagliolini according to packet instructions until al dente. Drain, return to the warm pot and toss with the olive oil and salt.

Spoon the red pepper sauce over the warm pasta and, if you like, garnish with Parmesan shavings. Pass the pepper grinder over each plate, grinding furiously before serving!

ABOVE RIGHT: *An old iron pot full of spoons for sale.*
Recommended wine: Fleur du Cap Unfiltered Voignier

Tomato & olive sauce

This light, fresh sauce is wonderful with fish. Enough to spoon generously over 6 portions.

- 250 g small black olives, pitted
- 100 ml olive oil
- 50 ml lemon juice
- 2 t coriander seeds, lightly crushed
- handful sage leaves
- 2 ripe tomatoes, skinned, seeded and chopped

Heat the olives gently in the oil, and then squeeze in the lemon juice. Remove from the heat and add the coriander and sage. Finally stir in the tomato, and spoon over the cooked fish fillets. Serve immediately.

ABOVE RIGHT: *Teapots anyone?*

BELOW: *Good enough to eat.*

BROCANTE ON A SUNDAY

Pavlova with strawberry syrup

What a lovely alternative to the normal pavlova. Hubert Maetz, a French chef with whom I've spent some time in the Alsace, always trained us by pointing out the 'cinema' factor... he would love this! Serves 6.

- 350 g egg whites
- 450 g castor sugar
- 1 T cornflour
- 1 t vanilla paste
- 750 ml white wine
- 250 ml castor sugar
- 1 punnet strawberries
- 1 t vanilla paste
- 300 ml thick cream

Beat the egg whites until soft peaks form. Take care not to whip them until they dry out - that will make the cooked pavlova brittle. Add half the sugar, spoon by spoon, beating all the time. Add the cornflour, then fold the rest of the sugar into the mixture. Make sure the sugar has dissolved, and finally add the vanilla.*

Spoon the mixture onto a large metal or ovenproof tray lined with greaseproof paper. I usually smear some unsalted butter over the greaseproof paper as well. Shape the meringue into a small circular pavlova… try to get as much height as possible, and to form a little 'hill' right in the middle of the pavlova that is not higher than the sides.

Place in a really warm preheated oven (about 220°C/Gas 7) and immediately reduce the heat to 140°C/Gas 1. Bake for about 2 hours. The pavlova will rise slowly and turn a light caramel colour with a crisp meringue look. The inside will be light and fairycake-like. Remove from the oven and let cool.

Bring the wine and castor sugar to a fast boil in a deep pot, and let it reduce to a syrupy consistency. Add two strawberries to the syrup. Add the vanilla paste and allow to cool.

Whip the cream until soft peaks form.

Just before serving, remove the strawberries from the syrup, which will be a lovely pink colour. Spoon the cream onto the cooled pavlova; heap the fresh, unhulled strawberries on top of the cream; and spoon the lovely pink syrup over.

* *Vanilla paste is fairly new in South Africa but can be found at most delis.*

Pesto

Delicious with fish, fresh tomatoes, or even dolloped into a bowl
of avocado soup. Makes about 200 ml.

- 150 g basil leaves
- 30 g pine nuts, roasted lightly
- 2 cloves garlic, roasted until soft
- 60 ml extra virgin olive oil
- freshly ground black pepper
- sea salt

Put all the ingredients into a food processor, and blend into a rough paste. Transfer to a bowl and serve.

Mayonnaise

What would life in France be without mayonnaise?
This makes about 350 ml.

- 2 egg yolks
- 10 ml creamy mustard
- sea salt and freshly ground black pepper
- 250 ml extra virgin olive oil
- 50 ml lemon juice

Whisk together the egg yolks, mustard and a little pinch of salt and pepper. Slowly pour in the oil, in a thin, steady stream, whisking continuously at a gentle pace. When it is incorporated, whisk more vigorously to make a thick mayonnaise.* Add the lemon juice to bring some zestiness to the mayonnaise and whisk.

* If at this point you add the pulp of 3 garlic cloves to the mayonnaise, you will have a superb aïoli to serve with soups or vegetables.

Oyster soup

This is a very fast, fabulous, cheap soup. One of those that even chefs have up their sleeves for an emergency! Serves 4 small starter portions.

- 1 tin mushroom soup, preferably Campbell's
- 1 tin smoked oysters
- 250 ml double cream
- 50 ml dry sherry
- 50 g flat-leaf parsley, chopped
- freshly ground black pepper

Heat the soup in a small saucepan. Halve the oysters and add, along with the cream and sherry. Stir gently whilst heating the soup. Do not boil. Spoon into warmed soup bowls and garnish with the parsley after a nice, solid grind of the pepper mill... voila! Serve with a slice of crusty brown bread.

'No one who cooks, cooks alone. Even at her most solitary a cook in the kitchen is surrounded by generations of cooks past, the advice and menus of cooks present, the wisdom of cookbook writers.' LAURIE COLWIN

CHAPTER 7

UX JARDINS DES THÉVENETS

The fountain that's permanently spouting crisp spring water is but one of the eclectic charms of the grand old lady that is Jardin des Thevenets. She's a farm on the edge of the Bourbonais region of the Allier in the Auvergne, with a 17th century farmhouse situated halfway up a small wooded hill, and surrounded by five hectares of woodland and almost as much of aromatic and medicinal fields. Espinasse Vozelle, the closest village, is a winding 10 minute drive from Vichy.

Driving on the little dirt road through the massive trees en route to the house, you're struck by the unspoiled countryside… until you realise that the fields around you are actually covered, depending on the time of year, by cornflowers, borage, blackcurrant, peppermint, sage and, in early spring, the tiniest, deep purple artichokes. There's a strong urge to immediately fill a basket and bake them in a copper pan with olive oil and a couple of handfuls of baby tomatoes. Once we walked through a mint field, bravely followed up the hill by the plump house cat, to a lone pear tree to find dessert… a heady experience.

This is a wonderful place to stay for a couple of days in one of the sensitively restored bedrooms, to go for restorative walks and swim in the large pool in what used to be a barn for horse-drawn carriages. Come evening, everyone sits down with the owners to an elegant organic dinner prepared by the hostess, who just happens to be a brilliant cook. Truly a privilege! ⚜

Avocado soup

On a warm summer day under an ancient Sophora Japonicus, this is what you want to enjoy as a cool, soothing starter. This soup is delicious... Serves 8.

- 1,5 ℓ chicken stock
- 125 ml cream
- 3 ripe avocado pears
- 1 ℓ Bulgarian yoghurt
- 1 onion, finely chopped
- 1 lemon, juiced
- seasoning

Bring the stock to a brisk boil and reduce by a third, until you have about a litre left. Add the cream, and just before it comes to the boil again, remove from the heat and chill. Peel the avocado pears, remove the pips, and pop them into a liquidiser with the yoghurt, onion and lemon juice. Blend until smooth, and pour into a mixing bowl. Slowly fold the cream and stock mixture into the avocado cream. Season and serve in individual bowls with a dollop of yoghurt as garnish.

RIGHT: *The beautiful homestead at Aux Jardins des Thévenets.*
FAR RIGHT: *The old gatehouse.*

ABOVE: *It's mostly edible!*

Tomato tarts

*Let's join the ongoing tide of tomato tarts! This one is really good though… and easy to make.
For a refreshing change I've on occasion made a single tart using a large flan dish. I use exactly
the same method and ingredients. Just adjust the amount of tomatoes in order to fill the dish
completely. This looks wonderful served on a platter lined with fresh rocket. Serves 6.*

- 1 sheet puff pastry, thawed
- 2 leeks, chopped and lightly sautéed in butter
- 125 g Roquefort cheese, sliced
- 100 ml egg mayonnaise
- 30 red cherry tomatoes

Preheat the oven to 220°C/Gas 7. Cut the pastry into rounds that will fit snugly into greased loose-bottomed flan dishes. Prick the bases with a fork and divide the fried leeks between them. Place a slice of cheese onto each layer of leeks. Spoon a small dollop of mayonnaise on top of the cheese, and follow that with five whole tomatoes for each tart.

Bake the tarts in the preheated oven for about 20 minutes. The puff pastry will rise beautifully around the filling and become a caramel color.

Serve straight from the oven with a crisp salad.

ABOVE RIGHT: *An old water pump.*

Recommended wine: Bain's Way Voignier

Fish with a herb & wine marinade

This is particularly great with both yellowtail and tuna, but works with almost all line fish. Serves 6.

- handful sprigs rosemary, chopped
- 1 sprig fennel, chopped
- 8 sprigs flat-leaf parsley, chopped
- 100 ml dry white wine
- juice of 1 large lemon
- 1 t sugar
- 3 cloves garlic, crushed
- 250 ml olive oil
- 2 bay leaves
- 6 pieces line fish
- salt and freshly ground black pepper
- 1 T cream (optional)

Recommended wine: Harvest Moon Sauvignon Blanc

Put the fresh herbs into a blender along with the wine, lemon juice, sugar, garlic and 175ml olive oil. Liquidise. Add the bay leaves.

Dry the fish fillets and season them. Pour some of the marinade in a flat dish, put the fish fillets into the mixture and pour the rest over the fish. Leave for at least an hour.

Drain the fish. Heat the remainder of the oil. Fry the fish until done. Remove from the pan and keep warm. Add the marinade to the pan and reduce by half. Strain the sauce, add cream if you want to, pour over the fish and serve.

Peach & caramel tarts

During summer, with an abundance of fresh fruit available, this is one of the handiest recipes around. Using a huge variety of soft fruits, I'm constantly churning out these little pastries. I use any fruit from apples to peaches, pears, prunes, you name it... Enjoy! Serves 6.

- 250 g sugar
- 125 ml crème fraîche
- 125 g unsalted butter
- 1 sheet puff pastry, thawed
- 100 ml butter, melted
- 6 peaches, each cut into 6 wedges
- 6 sprigs thyme

ABOVE RIGHT: *The rustic sitting room.*

Butter shallow individual flan dishes. Combine the sugar with 125 ml water in a saucepan, and cook over high heat until it turns a caramel colour. Add the crème fraîche, whisking vigorously. Be careful of the steam! Remove from the heat, cut the butter into small pieces and whisk into the caramel.

Prepare the pastry cases by rolling open the puff pastry, and cutting each sheet into 6 blocks with a sharp knife. Place the pastry blocks into the buttered moulds. Arrange the peach wedges in the cases.

Pour the caramel over, and bake at 220°C/Gas 7 for about 15 minutes until the pastry is slightly browned. Serve with a dollop of crème fraîche and a sprig of thyme for garnish.

Marinated olives with feta cheese

Make this at least the day before... the olives just get better with a few days in a fridge.
Serve with fresh bread. Makes enough for 4.

- 2 lemons

- 4 sprigs parsley

- 2 sprigs fresh rosemary

- 2 sprigs fresh thyme

- 2 cloves garlic, peeled and sliced

- 2 fresh bay leaves

- 120 ml extra virgin olive oil

- freshly ground black pepper and sea salt

- 400 g small olives

- 4 thick slices or rounds of feta cheese

Zest the lemons in thick strips with a potato peeler. Snip the parsley, rosemary and thyme into small pieces. Stir together with the garlic, bay leaves, olive oil and seasoning to taste, then add the olives and marinate overnight.*

To serve, put the feta on a pretty plate and pour the olives and the marinade over.

* I've found that the olives are delicious if I heat them slightly in the olive oil before adding the rest of the ingredients for the marinade. Try it.

ABOVE RIGHT: *Glasses and plates drying in the kitchen.*

Chicken with tomatoes & baby onions

I know that saying this is an old family recipe is rather boring... but in this case it is actually true. This is the dish my mom made for a heap of guests when my son was christened. It's really an old favourite and intensely heart warming! Serves 6.

- 100 ml extra virgin olive oil
- 150 ml plain white flour
- 60 ml paprika
- sea salt and freshly ground black pepper
- 1 free-range chicken, portioned
- 20 small baby onions, peeled
- 2 green peppers, grilled, peeled and pitted
- 2 cloves garlic, peeled and chopped
- 5 very ripe tomatoes, peeled and pitted
- 50 ml salted butter
- 20 small fresh mushrooms
- fresh parsley and basmati rice to serve

Heat the olive oil in a flameproof casserole. Mix the flour, paprika and seasoning gently, and sieve it over the chicken pieces. Brown them. Add the baby onions to the casserole with the chicken. Slice the green peppers in strips and add to the pot. Add the garlic. Slice the tomatoes in strips over a bowl to catch the juices, and add it all to the casserole. Do remember to remove the tomato pips... they are the culprits that can cause a tomato and chicken casserole to go sour. Add enough water to allow for some happy simmering - cooking should take just about an hour.

While that's going on, melt the butter in a pan and allow it to brown to make beurre noisette or nut butter. Add the mushrooms, and fry until they have caramelised.

To serve, pour the mushrooms over the dish, and garnish with a handful of freshly picked parsley. Have basmati rice on the side.

LEFT: *Enter through these stately gates.*

ABOVE: *Purple cornflowers.*

White chocolate mousse

The sexiest little mousse imaginable! Serves 8.

- 3 x 100 g slabs of white Lindt chocolate
- 375 ml cream
- 2 t pure vanilla bean paste
- 1 bottle light white wine
- 500 g castor sugar
- 16 strawberries (2 per person)

Place all the chocolate in a heat-resistant bowl and melt in a microwave at the lowest power for 30 seconds at a time, stirring frequently, until the chocolate is nice and smooth. In the meantime, beat the cream until it forms soft peaks. Stir in the vanilla. Stir the melted chocolate into the cream mixture with a spoon, and spoon the mixture into pretty glasses. Leave in a cool place (not the fridge!).

Boil wine and sugar until it is syrupy. Quickly dip the strawberries into the syrup and arrange them on serving plates, alongside the glasses of mousse. Drizzle with the wine syrup. Finger licking is totally allowed!

Venison in red wine & chocolate sauce

I always prepare the prunes at least five days ahead, and marinate the joint of meat for two days. This is a really old recipe that originates from Italy. In France I use wild boar, but venison works equally well and is much easier to come by in South Africa. I like to use the shoulder of the meat, because bones always add character to the sauce. Serves 10 if you're using the leg and 6 if you're using the shoulder.

Marinade

- 100 ml olive oil
- 125 g diced pork belly
- 2 carrots, peeled and sliced
- 2 leeks, sliced and rinsed
- 1 t dried sage
- 3 bay leaves
- 1 bouquet garni (see page 59)
- 4 cloves garlic, chopped
- 750 ml good quality red wine

Heat the olive oil in a large casserole and gently fry the pork belly until the fat runs. Add the carrots and the leeks and cook them gently. Add the herbs and the garlic and heat through. Add the wine and bring to a gentle boil. Allow the alcohol to evaporate… you will smell when it's all gone! It takes about 5 minutes.

Remove the liquid from the heat and let it cool down completely before you use it.

Place the venison into a huge lidded container. Pour the cooled marinade over the meat and cover. Turn the meat every 12 hours for 48 hours.

Recommended wine: Kanonkop Pinotage

RIGHT: *Wine glasses drying on the stone draining board that features a funnel that leads out the farmhouse kitchen window.*

Casserole

- 1,25 kg venison, trimmed
- 100 ml olive oil
- 1 carrot, peeled and sliced
- 1 leek, peeled and chopped
- 1 t dried sage
- 2 cloves garlic, chopped
- 2 bay leaves
- 1 bouquet garni (see page 59)
- 750 ml good quality red wine
- 100 g dark chocolate, grated
- 125 ml cream
- 125 g pine nuts, roasted
- 250 g dried, brandy soaked prunes*

* Remove the pips from the prunes and put them into a jar. Fill the jar with excellent brandy - you should not have any other kind in your cupboard! - before sealing the jar. Let the prunes soak for at least 5 days before you need to use them.

Heat the olive oil in a casserole that is big enough to hold the whole piece of venison. Fry the carrot and leek. When you're ready to cook, remove the venison from the marinade, and dry with absorbent paper. Pour the marinade through a sieve and keep the liquid.

Seal the venison on all sides in the hot olive oil before adding the sage, garlic, bay leaves and bouquet garni. Pour the strained marinade and red wine over the meat. Bring the liquid to a steady boil and simmer for about 2 hours. The liquid should be reduced by half and the meat soft. Remove the meat from the heat, put it on a platter and let it rest before slicing it thinly.

Bring the liquid to a fast boil and reduce until it has a thick, saucy consistency. Turn the heat down and stir the grated chocolate into the sauce. Add the cream and the pine nuts. Add the prunes to the sauce and allow it to heat through. Spoon the sauce over the meat. Serve with polenta.

CHAPTER 8

PARIS VIGNETTES

Strolling down Boulevard St Germain in the 7th arrondissement of the City of Light, I find it difficult to decide what pleases me most… the prospect of the haute couture of Sonia Rykiel on my left, or enjoying a tantalising ice cold Ricard at Deux Magots on my right. Hemingway knew what he was on about when he referred to the latter, Brasserie Lipp and Café de Flore, as 'a movable feast'!

Before reaching the Seine, I turn into Rue Jacob, passing the massive graffiti that is the epitaph to Serge Gainsborough on my way to lunch at No 35. A day in Paris is worth nothing without dejeuner. And after the last verre rouge - glass of red - a brisk stroll next to the river is called for. I look for the beautiful wooden-decked pont, the Passarelle des Arts, which connects the France Institute and the Louvre with a view of the Pont Neuf, Ile de la Cité and the Gothic mass of the Notre Dame.

It's always worth taking a walk, too, to St Paul's. On the way down the Rue de Rivoli, I slip down a side road and am intoxicated every time by the variety that is the Marais. These ancient, narrow lanes are lined with the most exquisite fashion, food and lifestyle boutiques alongside typical neigh-bourhood corner shops.

Early evening, I join the crowd that spills down Rue des Rosiers, past the shoemaker who loves reading Deon Meyer (in French, of course), and into Rue Vieille du Temple. Around the corner, in a surprisingly large courtyard, is Tresor, an eclectically decorated restaurant that's worth the trip to Paris all on its own.

Tomorrow, on the way to Charles de Gaulle and Cape Town, I'll stop at Laduree for pistachio macaroons, and at Bonne Marche in the Rue du Bac for the most wonderful herbs and spices from Albert Menes, not forgetting a bag full of the grey salt from Guerande...

Au revoir. ⚜

Salad of baby potatoes & oysters

Serves 6 - or one, if you're feeling really, really hungry for something that's going to speak to your soul.

- 20 waxy baby potatoes, peeled
- 5 ml salt
- 125 ml chicken stock
- 125 ml cream
- 6 spring onions, chopped
- 125 g unsalted butter, melted and set aside
- 24 freshly shucked oysters, drained
- sea salt and freshly ground black pepper

Recommended wine: Stellenzicht Chardonnay

Put the potatoes in a large pot of cold water, add salt, and bring to a slow, rolling boil. Cook until tender. Drain. Pour the chicken stock and cream into a medium pot and bring to the boil. Reduce to half the original volume. The mixture will be fabulously creamy. Add the chopped spring onion, and infuse and reduce a little more.

This salad needs to go straight to the table, so it's a good idea to warm 6 soup bowls and set them up. Warm the butter again over low heat and add the potatoes, tossing gently until they are coated and warmed up. Season to taste, and, with a slotted spoon, divide amongst the plates.

Remove the cream sauce from the heat and add the shucked oysters just to heat them through. Spoon the oysters and cream sauce over the potatoes and grind over a sprinkling of black pepper before serving.

Duck breast salad

Sage and duck marry like Marmite and toast. This is a stunner. Serves 8 as a starter.

- 10 sprigs fresh thyme
- 10 fresh sage leaves
- sea salt and freshly ground black pepper
- 2 whole duck breasts, deboned, with skin intact
- 50 ml goose fat
- 2 punnets rocket leaves
- 40 basil leaves

Vinaigrette

- 150 ml extra virgin olive oil
- juice of ½ lemon
- 50 ml castor sugar
- 5 ml creamy mustard
- sea salt and freshly ground black pepper

Chop the thyme and sage and in a small bowl, mix the herbs with the sea salt and pepper. Score the fat diagonally on top of the duck breasts. Using your fingers, rub the herb mixture into the slashes. Melt the goose fat in a very warm saucepan. Put the breasts, skin side down, into the pan and fast-fry until the skin turns a crisp brown. Turn the breasts over and fry for about 3 minutes, depending on how well done you like the meat.

Remove the breasts from the heat and let rest whilst you toss the rocket and basil leaves together. Dress the salad with vinaigrette before arranging a little heap in the centre of each plate. Slice the breasts thinly and arrange around the salad.

VINAIGRETTE
Pour the olive oil and lemon juice in a mixing bowl. Add the sugar and mustard and whisk the vinaigrette until the sugar has dissolved. Season to taste and toss with the salad leaves.

Recommended wine: Stellenzicht Rhapsody

Peaches in a white wine syrup with Roquefort

Cooking these peaches is one of the most delightful things to do - a little like alchemy… Serves 6.

- 375 ml dry white wine
- 250 ml castor sugar
- 6 rosy-cheeked peaches
- 5ml vanilla paste
- 6 thin slices Roquefort cheese

Bring the wine and sugar to a gentle boil in a pot that's big enough to hold all 6 peaches, ideally in one layer. Add the vanilla paste. Once the sugar has dissolved, place the peaches unpeeled into the pot.* Allow to simmer until they are soft, then remove and place them in the fridge. Keep boiling the liquid until the consistency is syrupy.

Remove the peaches from the fridge just before serving and peel them. The peels should slip off beautifully. Place each peach on a plate with a slice of Roquefort cheese. Spoon a little of the syrup over each peach and slice of cheese.

* Boiling the peaches with the skin on turns the syrup a lovely pink color.

FAR LEFT: *A brilliant jewel of a flower shop.*

Ceviche

This is a deliciously fresh starter that I love to serve rolled up in fresh spinach leaves. Eat it with your fingers! Serves 6.

- 1 kg sashimi-quality firm white fish fillets
- 10 lemons, juiced
- 2 red onions, finely chopped
- 3 red chillies, seeds removed and finely chopped
- sea salt and freshly ground black pepper
- coriander leaves to garnish

Slice the fish thinly and put in a ceramic or glass bowl. Add the lemon juice, toss and cover. Allow the fish to 'cook' in the juice for about 25 minutes. Mix the onion and chilli together, season, and fold into the fish mixture. Serve garnished with the coriander.

'O unfathomable, inexhaustible Paris...' COLETTE

LEFT: *A narrow street in the Marais.*

Recommended wine: Dalla Cia Sauvignon Blanc

Pasta with tomatoes & basil

Everyone should have a quick, trusted little pasta dish in their repertoire for a really pleasant, fast meal... this is mine. Serves 4.

- 200 ml extra virgin olive oil
- 400 g cherry tomatoes, whole
- 40 basil leaves, plus a few extra for garnish
- 4 servings tagliolini
- sea salt and freshly ground pepper

Heat the olive oil in a pot and braise the tomatoes in the oil. They will swell gently and some will burst the skin, creating a very flavourful olive and tomato sauce. Do not stir. Take off the heat. Shred the basil leaves and stir them into the tomato and olive oil just before serving.

In the meantime, boil the pasta in salted water until cooked. Drain and divide into pasta bowls. Spoon the olive oil, basil and tomato mixture over, season and garnish with a whole basil leaf or two. Serve with crusty bread.

RIGHT: *Serge Gainsborough grafitti on Rue Jacob in the 7th arrondissement.*
Recommended wine: Flagstone Fish Hoek Rose

Roast chicken with green olives & prunes

This is a wonderful dish that I often serve at big, friendly gatherings. It's equally great at room temperature. Serves 24.

- 2 heads garlic

- 125 ml extra virgin olive oil

- 50 ml balsamic vinegar

- 75 ml dried oregano

- 300 g pitted prunes

- 300 g pitted green olives

- 250 ml white wine

- 125 ml capers

- 5 free-range chickens, portioned

- seasoning

- 125 ml coriander, chopped

Recommended wine: Plaisier de Merle Chardonnay

The day before, pour a little olive oil over the garlic heads, wrap them in foil and bake them in a warm oven at 180°C/Gas 4 for 15 minutes or until soft. Squeeze the garlic out of the peels and whisk into the rest of the olive oil and the balsamic vinegar. Add the oregano, prunes, olives, white wine and capers. Put the chicken portions in a layer in a big oven dish and season. Spoon over the garlic mixture, cover and refrigerate overnight.

Heat the oven to 180°C/Gas 4, cover the dish with a lid of foil, and bake for about an hour, or until the chicken is well cooked. Arrange on a lovely platter, and spoon the olives, capers and prunes over the food using a slotted spoon. Garnish with the chopped coriander and serve.

'We'll always have Paris.'

HUMPHREY BOGART TO INGRID
BERGMAN IN *CASABLANCA*

ABOVE: *View of the Seine and the Louvre.*
FAR LEFT: *The arches leading to Pei's pyramid inside the huge
courtyard at the Louvre.*

Moroccan lamb with tomatoes & almonds

This is a fabulous dish to serve on a chilly night to a group of good friends. The honey is the secret! Serves 6.

- olive oil
- 2 kg lamb knuckles
- 2 big onions, quartered
- 2 cinnamon sticks
- 1 t ground ginger
- 1 t saffron
- 6 tomatoes, peeled and chopped
- 2 t ground cinnamon
- 4 T honey
- 2 cloves garlic, chopped
- sea salt and freshly ground black pepper
- slivered almonds to serve

Heat a little olive oil in a deep, heavy-bottomed pot, and brown the knuckles. Remove and set aside. Add the onions, cinnamon sticks, ginger and saffron to the oil. Toss the onions with the spices until they are slightly cooked. Put the knuckles back into the pot. Drain the chopped tomatoes through a sieve into the pot, and set the pulp aside.

Steam the knuckles in the tomato juice for 2 minutes before adding enough water to cover. Stew the meat over a low heat - you'll need something between 60 and 90 minutes - until tender. Remove the meat and cinnamon sticks; discard the latter. Add the chopped tomatoes, ground cinnamon, honey and garlic to the sauce in the pot and simmer for 3 minutes. Return the knuckles to the sauce and reheat. Season to taste.

To serve, garnish with a handful of lightly-grilled slivered almonds. The dish is delicious with couscous.

THE RIGHT TWO REDS 2003

SOUTH AFRICA

Recommended wine: The Right Two Reds

CHAPTER 9

EAGULLS AND VINEYARDS

On the other side of False Bay, not far from L'Agulhas on the southernmost tip of the continent, lie the farms of Blomfontein, Uintjieskraal and Geelrug. It is here, with the shadow of Soetanysberg on the horizon, that the sauvignon blanc and shiraz vineyards of Agulhas Wines grow in the crisp sea air off the icy Benguela.

This is a place of long white beaches and needle sharp rocks, wild winds and shipwrecks. It is also here that you'll find the brilliant white King Protea growing high on the mountain amongst the fynbos and a herd of springbuck drinking from the freshwater spring in front of the thatched stonewalled farmhouse of Brandfontein. And late afternoon, with a couple of freshly caught galjoen done over the coals, a glass of wine in your hand and with your eyes on the far dune on the other side of the bay, you know that, in Africa, you are blessed.

On the western slopes of Papegaaiberg in the Stellenbosch wine region, crouch the verdant vineyards of Middelvlei. Two massive white stone columns mark the entrance to the farm with its long brick road that leads down to the homestead and sprawling cellar. It was here, rather late one evening, that I

LEFT: *Brandfontein's sprawling stone homestead with Soetanysberg behind.*

picked up a movement on the side of the road... a huge porcupine scuttled out of the headlights into the vines.

Middelvlei is a farm dreams are made of. It is a place of children and friends, fig trees and huge dams, ducks and geese, guineafowl, cows, pot bellied pigs, donkeys and tiny mountain goats, tortoises and rabbits. Chardonnay and sauvignon blanc, pinotage and merlot, shiraz, cabernet and tinta barocca grapes are grown here and it's with these that the internationally known wines are produced. On any given Sunday, lunch consists of barbecued snoek, crusty white bread and grape jam, pumpkin cakes and cinnamon. Local cheeses and small, white, sun-warmed figs... all washed down with a glass of Middelvlei Pinotage/Merlot. ⚜

Croutons with crème fraîche & olive oil

Serve on a platter as a snack before dinner, or plate for individual starters. I normally serve two croutons per person. This recipe serves 4.

- rocket
- 16 thin slices Parma ham
- 150 g Philadelphia cream cheese
- 100 g crème fraîche
- Maldon salt to taste, about 2,5 ml
- 8 slices rustic bread, toasted to make croutons
- 100 ml olive oil
- black pepper

RIGHT: *The side chimney at Brandfontein. Recommended wine: First Sighting Sauvignon Blanc*

Line a platter with rocket leaves and place the Parma ham on top. Mix the cheese, crème fraîche and salt in a bowl - a fork works well. Spoon the creamy mixture on top of the toast, and make a little hollow in the middle of the cheese. Place the croutons on the parma ham. Spoon the olive oil into the hollow, followed by a good grind of black pepper, and serve.

As a very tasty alternative to the olive oil, you could use a spoonful of basil pesto (see page 130) on each crouton.

SEAGULLS AND VINEYARDS

Galjoen done over the coals

The greatest luxury in the world is to sit on Brandfontein's deck with half a galjoen, a helping of sweet potatoes and a glass full of shiraz. Serves 4.

- 2 freshly-caught galjoen

- black pepper and salt to taste

- 2 limes

Recommended wine: First Sighting Shiraz

When you clean the fish, don't scrape it. The scales protect the meat from the intense heat of the coals when it is cooking.

Barbecue the fish over medium heat, turning halfway through. The entire cooking time should be approximately 20 minutes. Remove from the coals and season. Serve with slices of lime and sweet potatoes (see page 175).

Honeyed sweet potatoes

To be enjoyed with galjoen. Good enough for the gods... Serves 6.

- 8 sweet potatoes

- 50 g butter

- 50 g castor sugar

- 150 ml water

- 100 ml honey

Halve each sweet potato and place in an ovenproof dish. Put a thin slice of butter on each half. Sprinkle with the sugar. Add water to the pan just to cover the base. Cover with foil. Steam/bake the sweet potatoes at 180°C/Gas 4 for 20 minutes. Remove the foil. Spoon a dollop of honey over, and return uncovered to the oven for another 15 minutes. (Add a handful of cinnamon sticks to the pan for fabulous flavour.) The sweet potatoes should be caramelised and totally yummy! Serve with the galjoen (see page 173).

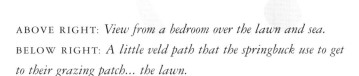

ABOVE RIGHT: *View from a bedroom over the lawn and sea.*
BELOW RIGHT: *A little veld path that the springbuck use to get to their grazing patch... the lawn.*

Spicy citrus cake

This is simply the easiest, must-have cake. It travels wonderfully for picnics and weekends away. Serves 10 with abundance.

- 500 ml self raising flour
- 175 ml castor sugar
- 2,5 ml salt
- 125 ml sunflower oil
- 5 eggs, separated
- 200 ml water
- zest of 1 orange
- zest of 2 limes
- 5 ml vanilla bean paste
- 5 ml powdered cinnamon
- 10 ml butter
- 50 ml icing sugar

RIGHT: *A table overlooking the sea.*

Recommended wine: Ambeloui Methode Cap Classique

Mix together the flour, sugar and salt. Add the oil, beaten yolks and cold water, and whisk well. Beat the egg whites until stiff peaks form, and fold into the batter with the orange zest, lime zest, vanilla bean paste and cinnamon.

Pour the batter into a large, buttered springform pan and bake at 180°C/Gas 4 for an hour or until a skewer comes out clean. Let the cake cool before removing it from the pan. Dust with a sprinkling of icing sugar.

Tabula noua partis Africæ

FIRST SIGHTING PAYS HOMAGE TO
BARTHOLOMEU DIAS,
maritime explorer, who left his native
PORTUGAL
in search of a trade route to the east around the tip of Africa.
IN THE YEAR 1488 HE FIRST SIGHTED
CAPE OF GOOD HOPE
thereby opening a gateway to a new world of
trade, which would have a profound influence
on Europe and the continent of AFRICA.

Apricot & pesto tarts

An artist friend was enjoying a sojourn in New York and called me when she was back in Cape Town, raving about this superb starter she'd had at a bistro. At the last tasting she declared that I'd just about got it right! Serves 6.

- 50 ml melted butter
- 30 apricot halves – fresh or tinned
- 25 g castor sugar
- 4 sheets phyllo pastry
- 250 ml fresh pesto (see page 130)

Heat the oven to 180°C/Gas 4. Butter a baking sheet with 20 g of the butter. Place the apricot halves on the sheet, sprinkle with the castor sugar, and bake for 25 minutes, until slightly caramelised.

Use the rest of the melted butter to lightly paint the phyllo pastry sheets, and cut each sheet in 6 squares. Fold the squares into six small flan pans (use four squares per tartlet). Spoon a dollop of pesto into each phyllo case and place 5 apricot halves, bottoms up, on top of the pesto. Pop back into the oven for 20 minutes or until the phyllo turns a light caramel colour. Serve as a starter with a green salad tossed in a light walnut oil dressing.

RIGHT: *Middelvlei homestead.*
FAR LEFT: *Harvesting chardonnay.*
Recommended wine: Middelvlei Chardonnay

ABOVE: *Using oak to age the wine.*

Venison pot pies

The most marvellous part of the aftermath of a hunting trip is the 'cooking off' of the bones. I have enduring memories of my boy-child perched on a barstool next to the kitchen table, sucking the marrow from the bones after I've scooped them out of the huge pot full of rillette or fynvleis. Serves 8.

- 50 ml olive oil
- 2 kg venison, off the bone (keep the bones)
- 3 pork trotters
- 750 ml dry red wine
- 500 ml chicken stock
- 2 carrots, peeled and sliced in pennies
- 1 celery stick, sliced with leaves
- 4 cloves garlic
- 2 leeks, sliced in pennies and rinsed
- 2 bay leaves
- 8 peppercorns
- 4 juniper berries
- 100 g butter
- 2 rolls puff pastry, thawed
- 1 egg

Heat the olive oil gently in your biggest pot. Fry the venison until it is slightly browned. Add the bones and the trotters. Pour the wine over the meat and bring to the boil. Add the chicken stock. Toss in the carrots, celery, garlic, leeks, bay leaves, peppercorns and juniper berries. Turn the heat down slightly, cover, and simmer for about 3 hours. The meat from the trotters should come off the bone, and the venison should be completely soft. Remove the meat and bones from the pot and reduce any leftover liquid. Let the venison cool slightly and shred it. Debone the trotters and combine the meats in the reduced stock. Season to taste.

Butter eight clay ramekins and divide the mixture between them. Roll open the thawed puff pastry and cut 4 ramekin-sized rounds out of each sheet. Place the pastry on top and over each ramekin, pinching gently with your fingers around the side of the dish in order to secure the dough. With a sharp knifepoint, make tiny criss-cross cuts into the dough to allow the steam to escape during cooking. Whisk the egg and brush the top of each pie to glaze.

Bake the pies for 25 minutes in an oven preheated to 220°C/Gas 7, until the pastry is a shiny, deep golden colour.

Serve immediately with gusto!

Recommended wine: Middelvlei Shiraz

Banon cheese with a green salad

Banon is a wonderful goatsmilk cheese that is matured in walnut leaves that have been soaked in white wine. I prefer to serve this on a slightly warmed plate... the cheese becomes runny and is delicious with the salad and a piece of baguette. Serves 8.

- 8 Banon cheeses
- baby spinach leaves, rocket and basil
- 50 ml olive oil
- 2 cloves garlic, chopped
- 5ml creamy mustard
- black pepper and salt

Place each Banon cheese on a plate. Toss the salad leaves together in a huge bowl. Whisk the olive oil, garlic and mustard together and season to taste. Pour the dressing over the greens and toss. Spoon the salad onto each plate and serve.

'A meal without wine is like a day without sunshine.'

JEAN-ANTHELME BRILLAT-SAVARIN

ABOVE RIGHT: *Figs and grapes served with brie makes for a great dessert.*
MIDDLE AND BELOW RIGHT: *Farm animals on Middelvlei.*
Recommended wine: Middelvlei Chardonnay

SEAGULLS AND VINEYARDS

Panna cotta with basil

Panna cotta is a universally loved dessert. A little touch of basil from the garden adds to the summery feel. Serves 6.

- 350 ml full-cream milk
- 250 ml single cream
- 5 ml vanilla paste
- 125 g castor sugar
- 2 gelatine leaves
- 125 ml double cream

Put the milk, single cream, vanilla and sugar into a pot and bring to the boil. Remove from the heat and fold in the gelatine. Stir until the leaves have melted. Strain the mixture through a sieve and let cool. Stir a little of this into the double cream before gently adding the latter to the milk mixture; strain again. Place a fresh basil leave at the bottom of each mould, and pour the panna cotta into the moulds. Chill until set. Turn out onto individual plates to serve.

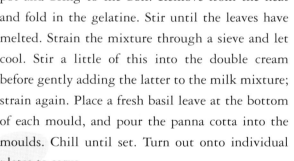

ABOVE FAR LEFT: *The first vineyard as you enter the gates...*

ABOVE RIGHT: *Empty bottles waiting to be filled.*

BELOW RIGHT: *Fermenting shiraz grapes.*

CHAPTER 10

THE ALLEY

Life in the Alley in Green Point Village has been likened to living in New Orleans or Notting Hill, and even the Marais in Paris, but, frankly, living here is unique. Where in the world do you still have a road sign that reads 'Up-and-Down Animal Drawn Transport Prohibited', hear the sound of foghorns and church bells, and children on skateboards in narrow streets; have fish vendors ringing your doorbell with the day's catch; and have on your patio a table under a fruit-bearing pomegranate?

This little village in Cape Town has its own character and soul, much of which centres around Piero's excellent coffee at the neighbourhood deli Giovanni's, where our children run up hot chocolate tabs for us to settle when we pick up the duck we ordered. We shop at the Tuesday and Friday organic market, and buy our Casablanca lilies from the wooden deck outside. There is also the corner shop where we pick up anything from firewood and puppy food to the morning newspaper and croissants. And then there's the story of the old man, the cellist and the prostitute...

Many a tale is told, sometimes in hushed tones, at long, leisurely lunches;

boisterous parties spill through the Alley onto the road; we trip over accordion players and saxophonists, mountain bikes and white-water kayaks. It's considered normal to carry a cooked meal up the road to share at a neighbour's table, bottle of robust red clutched under your arm…

Green Point Village is a place where life is lived. ❧

Thickly sliced salmon with horseradish cream

Having a chef-friend who supplies the most succulent, cold-smoked salmon is a gift. It was from him that I learned that thickly-sliced smoked salmon is truly the best way to enjoy it. Serves 6.

- 600 g whole smoked salmon
- 15 ml creamed horseradish
- 125 ml crème fraîche
- freshly ground black pepper to taste
- Maldon salt to taste

Place the salmon on a flat surface, and with a sharp knife, gently remove the skin. Slice the flesh thickly and arrange either on a platter or on individual plates. In a small bowl, gently fold the creamed horseradish into the crème fraîche. Add salt to taste.

Spoon the cream over the salmon slices and grind black pepper over. You can also spoon a little salmon caviar onto the cream.

This is also deliciously served with some avocado.

RIGHT: *The locals...*
Recommended wine: Stellenzicht Semillon

Gnocchi with green olives & Gorgonzola cream

I love serving this in old china plates around our yellowwood dining table, straight onto the old wooden top with crusty bread - and the ensuing crumbs! - amongst the wine glasses and bottles of red wine. The only linen is huge antique napkins. Serves 6 as a starter portion.

- 50 ml olive oil
- 1 red-skinned onion, peeled and chopped
- 100 g pitted green olives
- 250 ml chicken stock
- 250 ml cream
- 125 g creamy Gorgonzola cheese
- 5 ml coarse salt
- 500 g gnocchi
- 18 anchovies, drained
- 25 g salad onion, chopped

Heat the olive oil in a pot, add the onion, and gently fry it before adding the olives. Pour the chicken stock into the pot, bring to the boil, and reduce by half. Add the cream and the Gorgonzola, and gently stir until the cheese has melted. Remove from the heat.

Bring 2 ℓ of water to the boil in a pasta pot, and add the salt. Drop in the gnocchi, and scoop them out as soon as they rise to the top. Drop them directly into the warmed pasta dishes.

In the meantime, reheat the sauce, and add the anchovies. Spoon over the gnocchi. Sprinkle each dish with chopped salad onions, and serve immediately.

Recommended wine: Flat Roof Manor Cabernet Sauvignon/Sangiovese

Layered cheese with nuts & preserves

This recipe has been doing the rounds since my mother first served it about 25 years ago. I have adapted it over time, and it has even stood in as an appetiser on occasion. Serves 10.

- 1 Cambrieni cheese
- 500 g cream cheese
- 250 g mixed nuts, salted
- 10 preserved green figs
- 10 pieces preserved ginger

Halve the cheese horizontally and place the bottom half on a pretty platter; spoon 250 g cream cheese onto this. Thinly slice 2 figs and 4 pieces of ginger, and layer these on top of the cream cheese before replacing the top half of the Cambrieni, creating a 'sandwich'. Spoon the rest of the cream cheese on top, and sprinkle the nuts over, letting them spill onto the platter. Arrange the rest of the figs and ginger amongst the nuts on the platter and serve with biscuits.

ABOVE: *Fresh bread every morning.*
Recommended wine: Allesverloren Port

Fromage de chèvre tartlet

If you walk down the Alley, right at the bottom, on the left, you'll find a thick wooden door; and behind that door, under an ancient pomegranate tree, lies a tiny courtyard around an old stone fountain. This is where you'll find me serving light, tasty gems like these tarts to my fabulous friends. Serves 6.

- 1 roll puff pastry, thawed
- 50 ml butter
- 3 onions, peeled and sliced in rings
- 3 cloves garlic
- 15 ml fresh thyme, chopped
- 6 medium-sized Rosa tomatoes, sliced
- 1 chèvre, cut in even rounds
- 3 salad onions, chopped

Heat the oven to 220°C/Gas 7. Line 6 loose-bottomed tartlet pans with puff pastry. It is not necessary to thin the pastry - use it as it is, quite thick.

Melt the butter in a small pot and fry the onion rings until they are transparent. Add the thyme and cook for 5 minutes, making sure the onions don't burn. Remove from the heat and let cool a bit. Divide between the pastry cases. Place three slices of tomato in each tart, on top of the onion. Place a slice of chèvre right on top. Bake for 10 minutes, or until the pastry is crisp and golden. Sprinkle with the chopped onion, and serve with a light green salad as a starter. This is so good in summer…

To make sure the bottom of the pastry is not soggy, brush with a little egg white and pre-bake empty for 2 minutes. It works really well…

Recommended wine: La Cave Merlot

Fennel chicken cooked on a spit

During those grey, wet, wintry months in Green Point when the only given is the long low tones of the fog horn and the heaps of wood being carried in to feed the ever-hungry fireplaces, this slow-roasting chicken with its smell of sage and garlic is truly warming. Serves 10.

- 2 chickens, deboned
- 20 thin slices prosciutto
- 250 g pancetta - one piece
- 250 g prosciutto - one piece
- 6 cloves garlic
- 20 g sage leaves (dried) or 20 fresh leaves
- 2 t fennel seeds
- seasoning

After deboning the chickens, leaving all the meat attached to the skin, tuck in the meat of the legs and the wings and place the chickens, skin down, on top of the prosciutto slices. Coarsely chop the pancetta, prosciutto, garlic and sage all together. Transfer to a bowl and add the fennel seeds and seasoning. Spoon the chopped ingredients onto the prepared chickens. Roll the chickens with the prosciutto slices into tight rolls and tie each with five pieces of string.

Thread onto a skewer and fit it onto a spit. Cook for about 1 hour. Remove from the spit and let rest for 10 minutes before untying and discarding the string. Serve immediately with oven-baked potatoes with sage.

ABOVE RIGHT: *Fountain under the pomegranate.*
BELOW RIGHT: *A red Amarylla in the garden at the bottom of the Alley.*
Recommended wine: Flagstone Dark Horse Shiraz

'If the divine creator has taken pains to give us delicious and exquisite things to eat, the least we can do is prepare them well and serve them with ceremony.' FERNAND POINT

Saffron pears

This is a rich-looking and delicious-tasting dessert that is reminiscent of long, dusty journeys through exotic countries… Serves 6.

- 500 ml water

- 375 ml noble late harvest wine

- 50 ml castor sugar

- 2 cinnamon sticks

- 5 ml vanilla bean paste

- 10 ml saffron

- zest of 3 ripe oranges

- 6 pears, peeled, with stems intact

Bring the water and the wine to the boil in a pot big enough to hold six pears. Add the sugar and stir gently until it has dissolved. Add the cinnamon, vanilla, saffron and orange zest. Add the pears and turn the heat down slightly. Allow the liquid to simmer gently until the pears are cooked and soft, but still firm. Remove from the pot and keep aside. Reduce the liquid until it is a glossy, rich syrup. Spoon the syrup over the pears and serve with a dollop of double-thick cream.

ABOVE RIGHT: *Bright roses in a pewter bowl that I found at Green Point market.*

THE ALLEY

Mushroom soup with tapenade

Green Point Village is a place for soups. If you've just come back from a long walk on Sea Point Promenade in the bracing south-easter with the sea spray blowing in your face, this is what you need! Serves 6.

- 75 ml butter
- 500 g brown mushrooms, sliced
- 1 *ℓ* chicken stock
- 2 cloves garlic, peeled
- 250 ml thick cream
- Maldon salt to taste
- freshly ground black pepper to taste
- 30 ml crème fraîche
- 50 g tapenade

Melt the butter in a soup pot. Wait for it to brown - to become beurre noisette or nut butter - before adding the mushrooms. Fry the mushrooms over a high heat until the juices have cooked away, before adding the chicken stock. Bring to a rapid boil. Add the garlic. Reduce the heat and simmer until the liquid has been reduced by half. Remove from the heat and liquidise. Return the thick soup to the pot and reheat gently. Remove from the heat, fold in the cream, season and spoon into warmed soup plates. Drop a dollop of crème fraîche into the middle of each bowl followed by a spoonful of tapenade. Serve immediately - it's absolutely heart-warming with fresh crusty bread!

ABOVE RIGHT: *The old wrought iron gate in the courtyard of the Alley.*
BELOW RIGHT: *Glasses in the pantry... ready for use.*

"Laughter is brightest,
in the place where the food is."
-Irish proverb

Newport
market & deli
47 Beach Rd. Mouille Point. Tel. 021 439 1558

INDEX

BIBLIOGRAPHY

The Concise Larousse Gastronomique (Hamlyn, 2003)

Larousse Dictionnaire de Poche (Larousse/VUEF, 2002)

Collins English Dictionary (Collins, 1989)

Food Lover's Glossary of Culinary Terms (Culinary Software, 2003)

INDEX OF WINES

GLOSSARY

Albufera Anything 'a la d'Albufera' is so named after an original dedication to Antonin Careme to Marshall Suchet, Duc d'Albufera. Most commonly, chicken and duck dishes.

alfresco Outside, in the open.

bagna cauda Literally, 'warm bath'. A dip made of anchovies, olive oil and garlic, served warm.

beurre noisette Butter that has been gently heated in a frying pan until it is a dark golden colour and gives off a nutty smell.

bouquet garni A selection of aromatic herbs and plants, tied together in a small bundle and used to add flavour to sauces and stocks.

brocante Second-hand trade or antique market.

carpaccio An Italian dish made of paper-thin slices of beef, dressed with olive oil and Parmesan cheese.

chiffonade A very fine julienne of vegetables, usually associated with leafy herbs, lettuces or greens.

cognac A world-famous brandy distilled from wine, made in the region of Cognac, France.

coq au vin Chicken with bacon, onions, mushrooms, wine and flambéed brandy.

couscous A traditional North African dish made with semolina.

crème fraîche A cream to which a lactic acid has been added which thickens the cream, and gives it a distinctive sharp flavour without souring the cream.

daube A method of braising meat, usually in red wine stock.

flambé A French term meaning to pour spirits over food, then ignite it.

foie gras Goose or duck liver which is enlarged by methodically fattening the bird.

fromage de chèvre Goatsmilk cheese.

gremolata A mixture of chopped parsley, garlic and lemon peel.

infuse (ion) The process of steeping an aromatic substance in a boiling liquid until the liquid has absorbed the flavour.

julienne Cut into thin sticks.

pancetta Cured, unsmoked pork belly that is rolled and tied.

persillade A mixture of chopped parsley and garlic.

polenta Cornmeal porridge that is the traditional basic dish of northern Italy.

pot au feu An essentially French dish which provides at the same time soup, boiled meat and vegetables.

prosciutto An Italian word for ham, usually referring to the raw hams of Parma.

ragout A stew made from meat, poultry, game, fish or vegetables that is cooked in a thickened liquid and flavoured with herbs and seasonings.

reduce To concentrate or thicken a sauce or soup by boiling.

rillette A preparation of pork, rabbit, goose, game or poultry, deboned and cooked in lard and then pounded to a smooth paste, potted and served as a cold snack.

risotto A creamy Italian rice dish.

saffron A spice derived from the dried stigma of the saffron crocus. It has a pungent smell and a bitter flavour.

sauté To cook meat, fish or vegetables in fat until brown.

Sauternes A white wine from the Bordeaux region whose grapes are infected with noble rot, resulting in a rich, very fragrant and luscious wine. The most famous Sauternes of all is undoubtedly **Chateau d'Yquem**

soupçon An amount that is so tiny it is but a mere suspicion.

stock A flavoured liquid base for making a sauce, stew or braised dish.

strain To filter through either a strainer, colander or a cloth.

sweat To cook vegetables in fat over a gentle heat, so that they become soft and their juices are concentrated in the cooking fat.

T Tablespoon

t Teaspoon

tagliolini A flat ribbon pasta, narrower than tagliatelle.

tapenade A paste made of cured black olives, seasoned with olive oil, garlic, anchovies, capers and lemon.

vichyssoise A leek and potato soup thickened with fresh cream and served cold.

vol-au-vent A round case of puff pastry.

zest The coloured or outer rind of any citrus fruit.

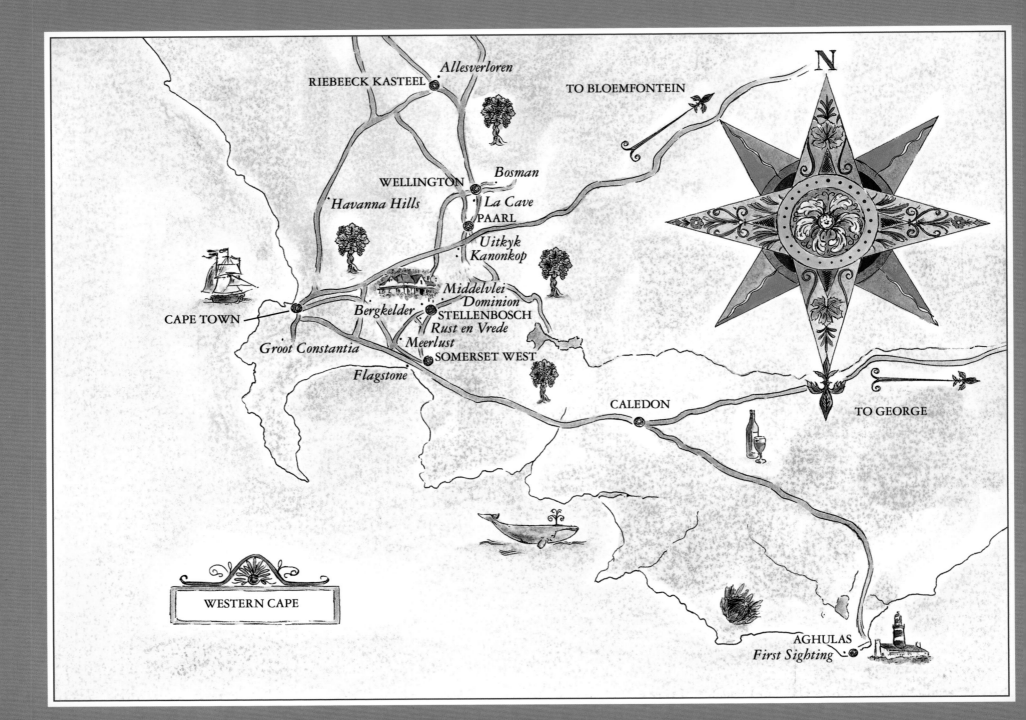